# Cuddly Crochet Plushies

## 30 Patterns for Adorable Animals You'll Love to Snuggle

### Glory Shofowora
#### Creator of Crafting in Glory

PAGE STREET
PUBLISHING CO.

PAGE STREET
PUBLISHING CO.

First published in 2024 by
Page Street Publishing Co.
27 Congress Street, Suite 1511
Salem, MA 01970
www.pagestreetpublishing.com

Distributed by Macmillan, sales in Canada by The Canadian Manda Group.

27   26   25   24            2   3   4   5

ISBN-13: 978-1-64567-876-2
ISBN-10: 1-645-67876-8

Library of Congress Control Number: 2023936575

Cover and book design by Molly Kate Young for Page Street Publishing Co.
Photography by Juliana Buenrostro, step-by-step photography
by Glory Shofowora

Printed and bound in the United States of America

To my mother and father,
who always show their
love and support
for all of my goals.

# Contents

# Introduction

When I learned how to crochet, I had the privilege of learning from my mother. I was 10 years old at the time, and I've continued to crochet ever since. Although I was taught how to crochet practical items like scarves, blankets and pillows, my mother didn't know the first thing when it came to crocheting stuffed animals. So, for that task, I had to learn on my own. I was shocked to discover that I could create stuffed animals similar to the ones commonly seen in stores! And it was more interesting than making shawls or clothing at 14 years old.

Crocheting patterns commonly seen on Pinterest was fun, until I realized that a huge majority of the patterns I encountered didn't have the "look" I was going for. I wanted my plushies to look cuddly and plush, and less rigid and anatomical. I wanted a more cartoonlike style, while other patterns strictly abided to the features and proportions of the animal, giving it a more basic design. I ultimately wanted to make plushies that emulated a feeling of childhood: bright saturated colors, untraditional body proportions and cuddly designs. And I felt like I could add my own personality through my plushie patterns, which was harder to do with shawls and clothing. I would challenge my skills and channel my creativity by crocheting my friends' favorite animals. Although I was able to

learn the basics through the internet, I wasn't able to buy patterns at the time. By my senior year of high school, I had started to share my original patterns with the world.

Crocheting is such a versatile skill: From tablecloths to pillows—if you can make it with yarn, you can crochet it. But some niche crochet projects are harder than others, and for some people this includes stuffed animals. The hardest part? Sewing too many tiny pieces together after making each one! Depending on the person, a plushie may end up in the work-in-progress basket in the corner of the room to be finished at a later time. This was a problem that I had too!

Throughout this book, you will learn not only 30 cute crochet stuffed animals you can make in a day or less, but you'll also learn techniques to eliminate the problems we often face when dealing with this niche. Do you hate sewing four legs to the body? Do you hate sewing multiple plates to the dinosaur you've been working on? Well, look no further! With the upcoming patterns, I hope to ease your struggles and make crocheting stuffed animals more enjoyable.

So, grab a hook, yarn and stuffing: You're going to create your own world of adorable animal plushies!

# Yarn to Use

Throughout this book, you'll notice I use the same type of yarn for each pattern: super bulky chenille yarn. You can buy this yarn through premieryarns.com, hobbii.com and amazon.com. Chenille yarn is different from basic acrylic yarn because it's made entirely of polyester. This specific yarn is created solely for making traditionally soft items, such as blankets, scarves and plushies.

I specifically use Premier® Yarns Parfait Chunky® for all of the projects you see in this book. Although this makes the softest plushies, this yarn isn't always available or desired for each person to use. Luckily, all of my patterns are designed in a way that proves even if you crochet using acrylic yarn, you will be able to have the same plushies at home! Chenille yarn is typically a super bulky weight, so aim for yarn in that weight size. Of course, the thicker and bigger your yarn, the bigger your plushie will be, and vice versa, so keep that in mind when choosing the yarn you'd like to use for your plushie.

Be sure to use the hook that your specific yarn recommends. I usually use a size 5mm hook for my projects, so you shouldn't have to stray more than 2mm above or below that for super bulky yarn!

# Beginner to Advanced: What's the Difference?

When it comes to the projects in this book, I've organized each pattern into an experience level that best suits the crocheter who would be able to successfully complete the project.

## Beginner

Beginner patterns have only one or two techniques used to make the plushie. When it comes to colors, expect to use one or two yarn colors max. There's not too much sewing involved (two or three pieces have to be sewn to create the final plushie), but any projects that require sewing need only the most basic sewing skills.

## Intermediate

Intermediate patterns have two or three techniques used to make the plushie. When it comes to colors, expect to use up to four yarn colors max. You will need to use your color-changing skills for these projects: crocheting x stitches in color A and x stitches in color B. Some sewing is involved (three to five pieces have to be sewn to create the final plushie), but the pieces that need sewing do not require advanced sewing skills. More embroidery for facial designs may be required. Oftentimes, a pattern stitch will be introduced.

## Advanced

Advanced patterns have three to five techniques used to make the plushie. Although the techniques aren't difficult, they may be daunting to an intermediate crocheter. When it comes to colors, expect to use up to four yarn colors max. As with the intermediate projects, you will need to use your color-changing skills for these projects: crocheting x stitches in color A and x stitches in color B. Sewing is involved (three to seven pieces have to be sewn to create the final plushie). The pieces that need sewing are not hard to sew themselves, but they are tedious. More embroidery for facial designs and other designs on the plushie will be required. Oftentimes, a pattern stitch will be introduced. Finally, these patterns will take the most amount of time, but advanced patterns in this book are far and few between, so don't fret about running into them too often.

# How to Crochet Limbs to a Body

Before you look at any part of the book, read this part! Almost every animal in this book utilizes this technique in one way or another.

When you work on a pattern, the round (Rnd) will say to "attach limb with x sts." In order to attach the limb properly to the body, place your hook into the x stitch (st) of the limb (images 1–2). For example, if the pattern says to attach the limb with 5 stitches (sts), place your hook into the 5th st of the last Rnd of the limb.

Then, place your hook into the next stitch of the body (image 3). At this stage, it's important that the wrong side (inside) of the body is facing up and the right side (outside) of the limb is seen, so that it will not be inside out.

Yarn over, and draw a loop through both sts (image 4). Then, yarn over and draw through both loops. Essentially, we're single crocheting (sc) the limb to the body (image 5). Repeat this for the remaining sts that the pattern specifies. To continue the beginning example, you would place your hook into the 4th st of the last Rnd of the limb and the next st of the body and sc them together (image 6).

Then, place your hook into the 3rd st of the last Rnd of the limb and the next st of the body and sc them together. Place your hook into the 2nd st of the last Rnd of the limb and the next st of the body and sc them together. Finally, place your hook into the 1st st of the last Rnd of the limb and the next st of the body and sc them together. Then, sc into the next sts of the body only, and continue to attach each limb the same way you did the first (images 7–9). Now you've got all of your limbs attached to the body and you didn't have to sew a thing! Now we can move on to the next Rnd.

(continued)

(Images Continued)

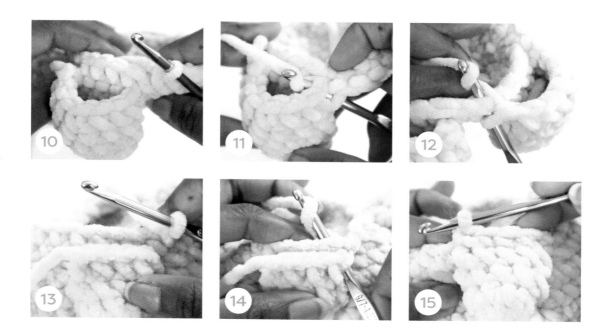

The next Rnd will say to "sc in the remaining sts of the limb." For a better visual, simply crochet in each of the stitches we didn't crochet in the previous Rnd (images 10–11). To continue on the previous example, if our limb had 16 sts total and we connected the limb to the body with 5 sts, we will crochet in the 15 sts left untouched. If you don't, you will end up with a hole—and we don't want that. Then, sc in the next sts of the body as stated (image 13).

For attaching limbs that have been single crocheted together, place your hook into the farthest st on the right side of the limb and the next st of the body (images 14–15). Then, sc the next sts together until you have attached the entire limb to the body (image 15). Continue to sc into the sts of the body.

# How to Embroider Eyes to a Face

In each of my plushies, you'll notice that there aren't any safety eyes used. That's because I embroider each and every eye onto all of them! Although this has its pros and cons, one huge pro is that the plushies made with embroidered eyes are safe for children. The common alternative is sewing on plastic "safety eyes," which are not actually safe for young children because they can pose a choking hazard if they come loose. So, if you're planning to make a plushie for a child, this section is for you.

First, cut a 12-inch (30.5-cm) strand of yarn from a color of your choice and put it through the eye of a tapestry needle. Poke your needle under the st you want to embroider the eye on, and through the top of the same st (image 1). Pull the thread through (but not all of it so you can sew the end into the piece later). Poke your needle through the same hole as before, layering your yarn on the left and on the right with every stitch (image 2). Continue to do this until you end up with a circle (images 3–4). This is the eyeball.

(continued)

Then, poke your needle through the side of the st on the right or left side of the eyeball you've made (depending on the side of the face you're working on) (image 5). Poke your needle next to the eyeball, making sure that it is at the midpoint of the eyeball (images 6–7). This is the eyelash. Sew in the remaining ends.

For the "sparkle" of the eye, cut a 12-inch (30.5-cm) strand of white yarn and put it through the eye of a tapestry needle.

Poke your needle through the eyeball at the top right corner (image 8). Then, poke your needle through the same hole that we used to complete the eyelash (image 9). Don't pull the yarn tight; you can place another needle in between the st to keep yourself from pulling the yarn too tight (image 10). Sew in the remaining ends.

This technique can be used with any yarn! Some yarn will take more stitches, and some will require less. Although this technique takes some practice, it's worth it if you'd like a different feel to your stuffed animals.

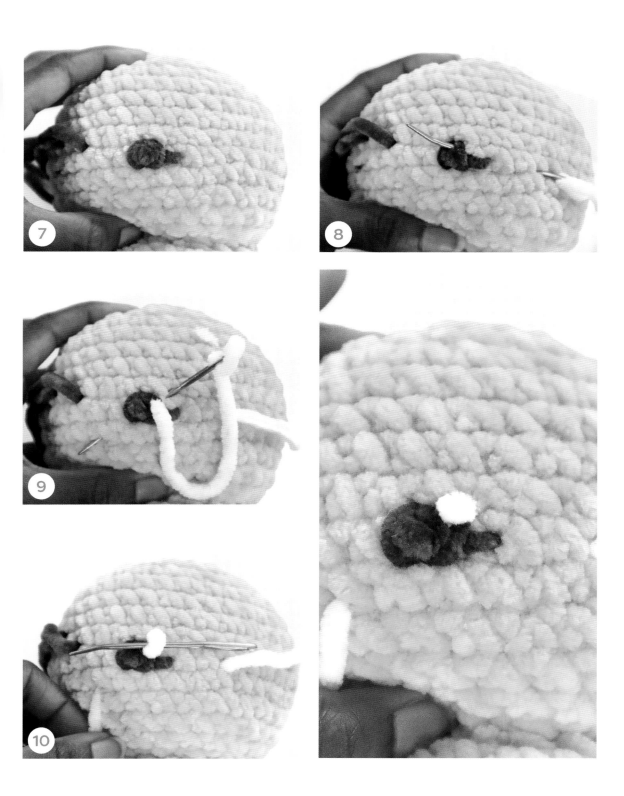

# Woodland World

Step into a mysterious and magical world within the forest! From sweet deer to cute bunnies, there is a wide range of animals that will connect to each individual's personality. Look carefully, and you can even see an adorable fox peek out from their den.

It's hard not to fall in love with these woodland critters! And what better way to bring them to life than through crochet? With each stitch and loop, you'll enjoy the journey, breathing life into your crocheted animals and discovering the pure bliss of crafting.

In this chapter, you'll be changing colors a lot! Many of these animals have distinct body colors that make them who they are, so having multiple colors of yarn will be a normal occurrence. To ease the difficulty of changing colors between stitches, I recommend not cutting the yarn after each color. Simply drop the color until you need it later, and then pick it up again when needed.

# Bella the Bunny

Bunnies are social animals—so you might need to make more than one. If you like minimal sewing, this pattern is for you! This bunny has a lot of facial shaping with a long strand of yarn to create the cute bunny head we all know and love; it's easier than you think!

**Skill Level**
Advanced

**Size**
Approx 12 inches (30.5 cm) long, 8 inches (20.5 cm) wide and 16 inches (40.5 cm) tall

**Yarn**
Super chunky chenille yarn, Premier Yarns Parfait Chunky, 100% polyester, 131 yds (120 m) and 3.5 oz (100 g) per skein

- Seashell (MC), 2 skeins, 262 yds (240 m) total

**Hooks**
US size H-8 (5mm)

**Notions**
Polyester fiberfill
Removable marker used to mark the first stitch of the round
Tapestry needle
Pair of 10mm safety eyes (optional)

**Gauge**
10 sc x 5 rounds = 4 inches (10 cm)

### Abbreviations

**Blo** = back loop only

**Ch(s)** = chain(s)

**Dec** = decrease (crochet 2 sc together)

**Flo** = front loop only

**Inc** = increase (work 2 sc into one stitch)

**MC** = main color

**Sc** = single crochet

**St(s)** = stitch(es)

## Left Back Leg

With MC, ch 2 and inc 3 times in the 2nd ch away from hook (6 sts).

**Rnd 1:** Inc in each st (12 sts).

**Rnd 2:** Sc in each st (12 sts).

**Rnds 3–5:** In the flo, inc 4 times. Dec 4 times (12 sts).

**Rnd 6:** Sc in each st (12 sts).

**Rnd 7:** (Inc, sc 2) 4 times (16 sts).

Fasten off and leave a 6-inch (15-cm) tail.

## Right Back Leg

With MC, ch 2 and inc 3 times in the 2nd ch away from hook (6 sts).

**Rnd 1:** Inc in each st (12 sts).

**Rnd 2:** Sc in each st (12 sts).

**Rnds 3–5:** In the flo, inc 4 times. Dec 4 times (12 sts).

**Rnd 6:** Sc in each st (12 sts).

**Rnd 7:** (Inc, sc 2) 4 times (16 sts).

**Rnd 8:** Sc 7. Leave the remaining 9 sts untouched for optimal leg attachment.

Fasten off and leave a 6-inch (15-cm) tail.

## Front Legs (make 2)

With MC, ch 2 and inc 3 times in the 2nd ch away from hook (6 sts).

**Rnd 1:** Inc in each st (12 sts).

**Rnds 2–6:** Sc in each st (12 sts).

Fasten off and leave a 6-inch (15-cm) tail.

## Tail

With MC, ch 2 and inc 3 times in the 2nd ch away from hook (6 sts).

**Rnd 1:** Inc 6 times (12 sts).

**Rnd 2:** Sc in each st (12 sts).

Fasten off and leave a 6-inch (15-cm) tail for sewing.

## Ears (make 2)

With MC, ch 13. Inc in the 2nd ch from hook, sc 10, and sc 4 in the last ch. Turn your work clockwise 180 degrees, so that you can work along the opposite side of the ch. Then sc in the next 10 chs, and inc in the last ch (28 sts).

**Rnd 1:** Inc, sc 12, inc in the next 2 sts, sc 12, inc (32 sts).

**Rnd 2:** Inc, sc 14, inc in the next 2 sts, sc 14, inc (36 sts).

**Rnd 3:** Inc, sc 16, inc in the next 2 sts, sc 16, inc (40 sts).

**Rnd 4:** Inc, sc 18, inc in the next 2 sts, sc 18, inc (44 sts).

**Rnd 5:** Inc, sc 20, inc in the next 2 sts, sc 20, inc (48 sts).

Fasten off and leave a 6-inch (15-cm) tail for sewing.

## Body and Head

With MC, ch 2 and inc 4 times in the 2nd ch away from hook (8 sts).

**Rnd 1:** Inc in each st (16 sts).

**Rnd 2:** (Inc, sc) 8 times (24 sts).

**Rnd 3:** Sc 4, attach Right Back Leg with 4 sts, sc 8, attach Left Back Leg with 4 sts, sc 4 (24 sts).

**Rnd 4:** Dec 2 times in the next sts of the Body, (dec 2 times, sc 8) in the remaining sts of the Right Back Leg, inc 8 times in the next sts of the Body, (sc 8, dec 2 times) in the remaining sts of Left Back Leg, dec 2 times in the remaining sts of the Body (40 sts).

**Rnds 5–7:** Sc in each st (40 sts).

**Rnd 8:** (Inc, sc 4) 8 times (48 sts).

**Rnd 9:** Sc in each st (48 sts).

**Rnd 10:** (Dec, sc) 4 times, sc 10, attach Front Leg with 3 sts, sc 3, attach Front Leg 2 with 3 sts, sc 5, (Dec, sc) 4 times (40 sts).

**Rnd 11:** Sc in the next 18 sts of the Body, then sc in the first 8 remaining sts of the Front Leg. Place your hook into the last remaining st of the Front Leg and the next st of the Body (3 sts on hook). Sc the sts together. Sc in the next st of the Body. Place your hook into the first remaining st of the Front Leg and the next st of the Body (3 sts on hook). Sc the sts together. Sc in the remaining 8 sts of Front Leg 2, then sc in the remaining 13 sts of the Body (50 sts).

**Rnds 12–14:** Sc in each st (50 sts). Stuff the Legs.

**Rnd 15:** (Dec, sc) 4 times, sc 26, (dec, sc) 4 times (42 sts).

**Rnds 16–18:** Sc in each st (42 sts).

**Rnd 19:** (Dec, sc 5) 6 times (36 sts).

**Rnd 20:** Sc in each st (36 sts).

**Rnd 21:** (Dec, sc 4) 6 times (30 sts).

**Rnd 22:** (Dec, sc 3) 6 times (24 sts).

**Rnd 23:** (Dec, sc 2) 6 times (18 sts). Stuff the Body as you work.

**Rnd 24:** Sc 8, inc 6 times in the flo, sc 4 (24 sts).

**Rnd 25:** Sc 8, (inc, sc) 6 times, sc 4 (30 sts).

**Rnd 26:** Sc 8, (inc, sc 2) 6 times, sc 4 (36 sts).

**Rnds 27–33:** Sc in each st (36 sts). If using safety eyes, attach them 11 sts apart on Rnd 31.

**Rnd 34:** (Dec, sc 4) 6 times (30 sts).

**Rnd 35:** (Dec, sc 3) 6 times (24 sts). Stuff the Head.

**Rnd 36:** (Dec, sc 2) 6 times (18 sts).

**Rnd 37:** (Dec, sc) 6 times (12 sts).

**Rnd 38:** Dec 6 times (6 sts).

Fasten off and sew the hole closed.

## Assembly

Sew the first 3 sts of the last Rnd of each Ear to Rnd 32 on opposite sides of the Head. Sew the Tail to the back of the Body, on Rnds 12–14.

Embroider a V-shaped nose in the middle of the face, lying between the midline of the eyes. Then, thread a 12-inch (30.5-cm) strand of yarn through the bottom of the Head, exiting through the intercept of the V-shaped nose, threading it 4 rows down vertically, and exiting through the bottom of the Head. Pull tight to indent the face, tie a knot, and weave in the ends. Weave in all ends.

Finish off the Head by threading a 12-inch (30.5-cm) strand of yarn up through the bottom of the Head, exiting through the left side of the eye on your left. Bring the needle 3 sts over, back through the right side of the left eye, and exiting through the bottom of the Head (see image 1 above). Bring the needle up through the bottom of the head, exiting through the left side of the eye on your right (see image 2 above). Bring the needle 3 sts over, back through the right side of the right eye, and exiting through the Head into the left side of the eye on the left (see image 3 above). You should have 4 sts on opposite sides with thread around them, and have both ends of the thread exiting the bottom of the Head. Pull tight to indent the face, tie a knot, and weave in the ends (see image 4 above).

If you prefer to embroider the eyes instead of using safety eyes, set them 11 sts apart on Rnd 32 of the Head (for more information on sewing eyes onto plushies, see page 13).

# Rae the Raccoon

Raccoons are nocturnal animals, making this plushie the perfect animal for nighttime cuddling! This raccoon may work slower than the other animals because it has a lot of colors in its fur. However, once you finish the final plush, the raccoon will stand out as one of your cutest creations!

## Skill Level
Beginner

## Size
Approx 12 inches (30.5 cm) long, 6 inches (15 cm) wide and 10 inches (25.5 cm) tall

## Yarn
Super chunky chenille yarn, Premier Yarns Parfait Chunky, 100% polyester, 131 yds (120 m) and 3.5 oz (100 g) per skein

- Light Gray (MC), 2 skeins, 262 yds (240 m) total
- White (C1), ½ skein, approx 66 yds (60 m) total
- Seal (C2), ½ skein, approx 66 yds (60 m) total
- Black (C3), ⅓ skein, 44 yds (40 m) total

## Hooks
US size H-8 (5mm)

## Notions
Polyester fiberfill
Removable marker used to mark the first stitch of the round
Tapestry needle
Pair of 6mm safety eyes (optional)

## Gauge
10 sc x 5 rounds = 4 inches (10 cm)

## Abbreviations
**Blo** = back loop only
**C1** = color 1
**C2** = color 2
**C3** = color 3
**Ch(s)** = chain(s)
**Dec** = decrease (crochet 2 sc together)
**Inc** = increase (work 2 sc into one stitch)
**MC** = main color
**Sc** = single crochet
**St(s)** = stitch(es)

## Legs (make 4)

With C2, ch 2 and inc 3 times in the 2nd ch away from hook (6 sts).

**Rnd 1:** Inc in each st (12 sts).

**Rnd 2:** Sc in the blo of each st (12 sts). Break C2.

**Rnd 3:** With MC, sc in the blo of each st (12 sts).

**Rnd 4:** Sc in each st (12 sts).

Fasten off and leave a 6-inch (15-cm) tail.

## Tail

With C3, ch 2 and inc 3 times in the 2nd ch away from hook (6 sts).

**Rnd 1:** Inc 6 times (12 sts).

**Rnds 2–3:** Sc in each st (12 sts).

**Rnds 4–6:** With MC, sc in each st (12 sts).

**Rnds 7–9:** With C3, sc in each st (12 sts). Break C3.

**Rnds 10–12:** With MC, sc in each st (12 sts). Stuff the Tail.

**Rnd 13:** Ch 1. Fold the Tail in half side to side, and sc across through both sides (for more information on sc across both sides, see Gale the Giraffe, page 59).

Fasten off and leave a 3-inch (7.5-cm) tail.

## Body

With MC, ch 10. Inc in the 2nd ch from hook, sc in the next 7 chs, and inc 2 times in the last ch. Turn your work clockwise 180 degrees, so that you can work along the opposite side of the ch. Then, sc in the next 7 chs, and inc in the last ch (22 sts).

**Rnd 1:** Inc in the first 2 sts, sc 7, inc in the next 4 sts, sc 7, inc in the last 2 sts (30 sts).

**Rnd 2:** (Sc 2, attach Leg with 3 sts, sc 5, attach the next Leg with 3 sts, sc 2) 2 times (30 sts) (for more information on attaching legs, see page 10).

**Rnd 3:** (Sc in the first 2 sts of the Body, sc in the remaining 9 sts of the Leg, sc in the next 5 sts of the Body, sc in the remaining 9 sts of the next Leg, sc in the next 2 sts of the Body) 2 times (54 sts).

**Rnd 4:** (Inc, sc 8) 6 times (60 sts).

**Rnds 5–10:** Sc in each st (60 sts).

**Rnd 11:** (Dec, sc 8) 6 times (54 sts).

**Rnds 12–14:** Sc in each st (54 sts). Lightly stuff the Body as you work.

**Rnd 15:** (Dec, sc 7) 6 times (48 sts).

**Rnds 16–17:** Sc in each st (48 sts).

**Rnd 18:** (Dec, sc 6) 6 times (42 sts).

**Rnd 19:** Sc in each st (42 sts).

**Rnd 20:** (Dec, sc 5) 6 times (36 sts). Stuff the Body.

**Rnd 21:** (Dec, sc 4) 6 times (30 sts).

**Rnd 22:** (Dec, sc 3) 6 times (24 sts).

**Rnd 23:** (Dec, sc 2) 6 times (18 sts).

**Rnd 24:** (Dec, sc) 6 times (12 sts).

**Rnd 25:** Dec 6 times (6 sts).

Fasten off and sew the hole closed.

## Ears (make 2)

With MC, ch 2 and inc 2 times in the 2nd ch away from hook (4 sts).

**Rnd 1:** (Inc, sc) 2 times (6 sts).

**Rnd 2:** With MC, sc 2. With C1, sc. With MC, sc 3 (6 sts).

**Rnd 3:** With MC, sc 2. With C1, inc. With MC, sc 2, inc in last st (8 sts).

**Rnd 4:** With MC, sc 2. With C1, sc, inc. With MC, sc 3, inc in last st (10 sts). Break C1.

**Rnd 5:** With MC, ch 1. Fold the Ear in half side to side, and sc across through both sides (6 sts) (for more information on sc across both sides, see Gale the Giraffe, page 59).

## Head

With C1, ch 2 and inc 3 times in the 2nd ch away from hook (6 sts).

**Rnd 1:** Inc 6 times (12 sts).

**Rnd 2:** (Sc 2, inc) 4 times (16 sts).

**Rnd 3:** Sc in each st (16 sts).

**Rnd 4:** With C1, sc 3. With C2, sc 3. With C1, sc. With MC, sc 2. With C1, sc. With C2, sc 3. With C1, sc 3 (16 sts).

**Rnd 5:** With C1, sc 3. With C2, sc, inc 2 times. With C1, inc. With MC, inc 2 times. With C1, inc. With C2, inc 2 times, sc. With C1, sc 3 (24 sts).

**Rnd 6:** With C1, sc 3. With C2, inc, sc 3, inc. With C1, sc 2. With MC, sc, inc, sc 3. With C1, inc. With C2, sc 3, inc, sc. With C1, sc 2, inc (30 sts). If using safety eyes, attach them on this round, 14 sts apart.

**Rnd 7:** With C1, sc 4. With C2, sc 5. With C1, sc 3. With MC, sc 7. With C1, sc 2. With C2, sc 5. With C1, sc 2. With MC, sc 2 (30 sts). Break C2.

**Rnd 8:** With MC, sc 3. With C1, sc 9. With MC, sc 8. With C1, sc 8. With MC, sc 2 (30 sts).

**Rnd 9:** With MC, sc 4. With C1, sc 8. With MC, sc 9. With C1, sc 7. With MC, sc 2 (30 sts). Break C1.

**Rnd 10:** With MC, sc in each st (30 sts).

**Rnd 11:** Sc 10, attach Ear with 5 sts, sc 4, attach Ear 2 with 5 sts, sc 6 (30 sts).

**Rnd 12:** (Dec, sc 3) 6 times (24 sts).

**Rnd 13:** Sc in each st (24 sts). Stuff the Head.

**Rnd 14:** (Dec, sc 2) 6 times (18 sts).

**Rnd 15:** (Dec, sc) 6 times (12 sts).

**Rnd 16:** Dec 6 times (6 sts).

Fasten off and leave an 8-inch (20.5-cm) tail. Sew the hole closed.

## Assembly

Sew the Head to the front of the Body on Rnds 16–21. Sew the Tail to the back of the Body on Rnd 17. Sew a triangle-shaped nose covering Rnds 1–3 of the Head (see images above). Weave in all ends.

If you prefer to embroider the eyes instead of using safety eyes, set them 14 sts apart on Rnd 6 of the Head (for more information on embroidering eyes, see page 13).

# Flynn the Fox

Although they look sly, foxes are actually friendly creatures. Work up this fox to make a new friend! This pattern includes the fluffiest tail—perfect for kids and adults alike. A friendy fox indeed.

**Skill Level**
Intermediate

**Size**
Approx 6 inches (15 cm) long, 4.5 inches (11.5 cm) wide and 10 inches (25.5 cm) tall

**Yarn**
Super chunky chenille yarn, Premier Yarns Parfait Chunky, 100% polyester, 131 yds (120 m) and 3.5 oz (100 g) per skein

- Tangerine (MC), 2 skeins, 262 yds (240 m) total
- Cream (C1), ½ skein, approx 66 yds (60 m) total
- Chocolate (C2), ⅓ skein, 44 yds (40 m) total

**Hooks**
US size H-8 (5mm)

**Notions**
Polyester fiberfill
Removable marker used to mark the first stitch of the round
Tapestry needle
Pair of 10mm safety eyes (optional)

**Gauge**
10 sc x 5 rounds = 4 inches (10 cm)

### Abbreviations

C1 = color 1
C2 = color 2
Ch(s) = chain(s)
Dec = decrease (crochet 2 sc together)
Flo = front loop only
Inc = increase (work 2 sc into one stitch)
MC = main color
Sc = single crochet
Sl st = slip stitch
St(s) = stitch(es)

## Legs (make 4)

With C2, ch 2 and inc 3 times in the 2nd ch away from hook (6 sts).

**Rnd 1:** Inc in each st (12 sts).

**Rnds 2–7:** Sc in each st (12 sts).

Fasten off and leave a 3-inch (7.5-cm) tail. Do not stuff.

## Tail

With C2, ch 2 and inc 3 times in the 2nd ch away from hook (6 sts).

**Rnd 1:** Inc 6 times (12 sts).

**Rnds 2–5:** Sc in each st (12 sts). Break C2.

**Rnds 6–10:** With MC, sc in each st (12 sts).

**Rnd 11:** (Dec, sc) 4 times (8 sts).

**Rnd 12:** Sc in each st (8 sts).

**Rnd 13:** Ch 1. Fold the Tail in half side to side, and sc across through both sides (4 sts) (for more information on sc across both sides, see Gale the Giraffe, page 59).

Fasten off and leave a 3-inch (7.5-cm) tail. Do not stuff.

## Ears (make 2)

With C2, ch 2 and inc 2 times in the 2nd ch away from hook (4 sts).

**Rnd 1:** Sc in each st (4 sts).

**Rnd 2:** With C2, inc. With C1, sc. With C2, inc, sc (6 sts).

**Rnd 3:** With C2, inc, sc. With C1, sc, inc. With C2, sc 2 (8 sts).

**Rnd 4:** With C2, inc, sc 2. With C1, sc, inc, sc 2. With C2, sc (10 sts).

**Rnd 5:** Ch 1. Fold the Ear in half side to side, and sc across through both sides (5 sts) (for more information on sc across both sides, see Gale the Giraffe, page 59).

Fasten off and leave a 3-inch (7.5-cm) tail. Do not stuff.

## Body

With C1, ch 10. Inc in the 2nd ch from hook, sc in the next 7 chs, and inc 2 times in the last ch. Turn your work clockwise 180 degrees, so that you can work along the opposite side of the ch. Then sc in the next 7 chs, and inc in the last ch (22 sts).

**Rnd 1:** Inc in the next 2 sts, sc 7, inc in the next 4 sts, sc 7, inc in the last 2 sts (30 sts).

 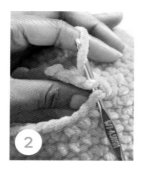  

**Rnd 2:** (Sc 2, attach Leg with 3 sts, sc 5, attach the next Leg with 3 sts, sc 2) 2 times (30 sts) (for more information on attaching legs, see page 10).

**Rnd 3:** (With C1, sc in the next 2 sts of the Body. With MC, sc in the remaining 9 sts of the next Leg. With C1, sc in the next 5 sts of the Body. With MC, sc in the remaining 9 sts of the next Leg. With C1, sc in the next 2 sts of the Body) 2 times (54 sts).

**Rnd 4:** With C1, sc 3. With MC, sc 9. With C1, sc 4. With MC, sc 10. With C1, sc 3. With MC, sc 10. With C1, sc 4. With MC, sc 7. With C1, sc 4 (54 sts).

**Rnd 5:** With C1, sc 4. With MC, sc 46. With C1, sc 4 (54 sts).

**Rnds 6–7:** With C1, sc 4. With MC, sc 47. With C1, sc 3 (54 sts).

**Rnds 8–9:** With C1, sc 5. With MC, sc 47. With C1, sc 2 (54 sts).

**Rnd 10:** With C1, sc 6. With MC, sc 47. With C1, sc (54 sts).

**Rnd 11:** With C1, sc 6. With MC, sc 48 (54 sts).

**Rnd 12:** With MC, sc. With C1, sc 4. With MC, sc 49 (54 sts). Break C1.

**Rnd 13:** With MC, sc 16, (dec, sc 3) 6 times, sc 8 (48 sts). Stuff lightly as you work.

**Rnd 14:** Sc in each st (48 sts).

**Rnd 15:** Sc 16, (dec, sc 2) 6 times, sc 8 (42 sts).

**Rnd 16:** Sc in each st (42 sts).

**Rnd 17:** Sc 16, (dec, sc) 6 times, sc 8 (36 sts).

**Rnd 18:** Sc 21. Place your hook into the flo of the 23rd and 22nd st (3 sts on hook) (see image 1 above). Sl st the sts together. Repeat this for the 24th and 21st st, the 25th and 20th st, the 26th and 19th st, the 27th and 18th st, the 28th and 17th st, the 29th and 16th st, the 30th and 15th st, the 31st and 14th st, and the 32nd and 13th st (images 2–4 above). Sc in the 33rd st, and the remaining 3 sts of this Rnd and the first 12 sts of the next Rnd. This is the new beginning of the Rnd (16 sts). Stuff the Body. Overstuff the Body on Rnds 16–18.

**Rnds 19–21:** Sc in each st (16 sts). This is the Neck portion.

Fasten off and leave a 6-inch (15-cm) tail for sewing. Finish stuffing the Body and Neck.

## Head

With MC, ch 2 and inc 3 times in the 2nd ch away from hook (6 sts).

**Rnd 1:** With MC, inc 4 times. With C1, inc 2 times (12 sts).

**Rnd 2:** With MC, sc 8. With C1, sc 4 (12 sts).

**Rnd 3:** With C1, sc. With MC, sc, inc, sc 2, inc, sc 2. With C1, inc, sc 2, inc (16 sts).

**Rnd 4:** With C1, sc 2. With MC, sc, inc, sc 3, inc, sc 2. With C1, sc, inc, sc 3, inc (20 sts).

**Rnd 5:** With C1, sc 3. With MC, sc, inc, sc 4, inc, sc 2. With C1, sc 2, inc, sc 4, inc (24 sts).

**Rnd 6:** With C1, sc 3. With MC, in the flo, (sc, inc) 6 times. With C1, sc 9 (30 sts).

**Rnd 7:** With C1, sc 3. With MC, sc 19. With C1, sc 8 (30 sts).

**Rnd 8:** With C1, sc 3. With MC, sc 20. With C1, sc 7 (30 sts). If using safety eyes, attach them on this round, 9 sts apart.

**Rnd 9:** With C1, sc 3. With MC, sc 21. With C1, sc 6 (30 sts).

**Rnd 10:** With C1, sc 3. With MC, sc 22. With C1, sc 5 (30 sts).

**Rnd 11:** With C1, sc 3. With MC, sc 23. With C1, sc 4 (30 sts). Break C1.

**Rnd 12:** With MC, sc 6, attach Ear with 5 sts, sc 4, attach Ear 2 with 5 sts, sc 10 (30 sts).

**Rnd 13:** (Dec, sc 3) 6 times (24 sts).

**Rnd 14:** Sc in each st (24 sts).

**Rnd 15:** (Dec, sc 2) 6 times (18 sts). Stuff the Head.

**Rnd 16:** (Dec, sc) 6 times (12 sts).

**Rnd 17:** Dec 6 times (6 sts).

Fasten off and sew the hole closed.

## Assembly

Sew the Head to the top of the Body. When aligning it to the Neck, make sure to sew Rnds 6–10 of the Head to the Neck. Embroider a triangle-shaped nose onto the face, covering Rnds 7–12 of the Head (see images 5–8 above). Sew the Tail to the back of the Fox's Body, approximately at Rnd 4. Weave in all ends.

If you prefer to embroider the eyes instead of using safety eyes, set them 9 sts apart on Rnd 8 of the Head (for more information on sewing eyes onto plushies, see page 13).

# Dari the Deer

Dari was inspired by a classic Disney character: Bambi. Like Bambi, this deer will tug at your heartstrings! The deer includes a little tail, perfectly sized for its round, squishy body.

**Skill Level**
Intermediate

**Size**
Approx 12 inches (30.5 cm) long, 9 inches (23 cm) wide and 9 inches (23 cm) tall

**Yarn**
Super chunky chenille yarn, Premier Yarns Parfait Chunky, 100% polyester, 131 yds (120 m) and 3.5 oz (100 g) per skein

- Toffee (MC), 2 skeins, 262 yds (240 m) total
- Seashell (C1), ½ skein, approx 66 yds (60 m) total
- Chocolate (C2), ¼ skein, approx 33 yds (30 m) total

**Hooks**
US size H-8 (5mm)

**Notions**
Polyester fiberfill
Removable marker used to mark the first stitch of the round
Tapestry needle
Pair of 10mm safety eyes (optional)

**Gauge**
10 sc x 5 rounds = 4 inches (10 cm)

## Abbreviations

**C1** = color 1

**C2** = color 2

**Ch(s)** = chain(s)

**Dec** = decrease (crochet 2 sc together)

**Flo** = front loop only

**Inc** = increase (work 2 sc into one stitch)

**MC** = main color

**Sc** = single crochet

**St(s)** = Stitch(es)

## Pattern Stitches

**Puff Stitch** = Yarn over, insert your hook through the st, yarn over and then draw up a loop. Repeat until you have 6 loops on the hook. Yarn over and draw through all 6 loops.

## Legs (make 4)

With C2, ch 2 and inc 3 times in the 2nd ch away from hook (6 sts).

**Rnd 1:** Inc in each st (12 sts).

**Rnd 2:** Sc in each st (12 sts).

**Rnds 3–5:** With MC, sc in each st (12 sts).

Fasten off and leave a 3-inch (7.5-cm) tail.

## Body

With C1, ch 10. Inc in the 2nd ch from hook, sc 7, and sc 4 in the last ch. Turn your work clockwise 180 degrees, so that you can work along the opposite side of the ch. Then sc in the next 7 chs, and inc in the last ch (22 sts).

**Rnd 1:** Inc in the next 2 sts, sc 7, inc in the next 4 sts, sc 7, inc in the last 2 sts (30 sts).

**Rnd 2:** (Sc 2, attach Leg with 3 sts, sc 5, attach the next Leg with 3 sts, sc 2) 2 times (30 sts) (for more information on attaching legs, see page 10).

**Rnd 3:** (With C1, sc in the next 2 sts of the Body. With MC, sc in the remaining 9 sts of the next Leg. With C1, sc in the next 5 sts of the Body. With MC, sc in the remaining 9 sts of the next Leg. With C1, sc in the next 2 sts of the Body) 2 times (54 sts).

**Rnd 4:** With C1, sc 3. With MC, sc 9. With C1, sc 4. With MC, sc 10. With C1, sc 3. With MC, sc 10. With C1, sc 4. With MC, sc 8. With C1, sc 3 (54 sts).

**Rnd 5:** With C1, sc 4. With MC, sc 47. With C1, sc 3 (54 sts).

**Rnd 6:** With C1, sc 5. With MC, sc 46. With C1, sc 3 (54 sts).

**Rnd 7:** With C1, sc 5. With MC, sc 47. With C1, sc 2 (54 sts).

**Rnd 8:** With C1, sc 5. With MC, sc 48. With C1, sc (54 sts).

**Rnds 9–10:** With C1, sc 5. With MC, sc 49 (54 sts). Break C1.

**Rnds 11–12:** With MC, sc in each st (54 sts).

**Rnd 13:** Sc 16, (dec, sc 3) 6 times, sc 8 (48 sts). Stuff lightly as you work.

**Rnd 14:** Sc in each st (48 sts).

**Rnd 15:** Sc 16, (dec, sc 2) 6 times, sc 8 (42 sts).

**Rnd 16:** Sc in each st (42 sts).

**Rnd 17:** Sc 16, (dec, sc) 6 times, sc 8 (36 sts).

**Rnd 18:** Sc 21. Place your hook into the flo of the 23rd and 22nd st (3 sts on hook). Sl st the sts together. Repeat this for the 24th and 21st st, the 25th and 20th st, the 26th and 19th st, the 27th and 18th st, the 28th and 17th st, the 29th and 16th st, the 30th and 15th st, the 31st and 14th st, and the 32nd and 13th st (for more information on closing off a body, see Flynn the Fox, page 29). Sc in the 33rd st, and the remaining 3 sts of this Rnd and the first 12 sts of the next Rnd. This is the new beginning of the Rnd (16 sts). Stuff the Body. Overstuff the Body on Rnds 16–18.

**Rnds 19–21:** Sc in each st (16 sts). This is the Neck portion.

Fasten off and leave a 6-inch (15-cm) tail for sewing. Finish stuffing the Body and Neck.

## Ears (make 2)

With MC, ch 2 and inc 3 times in the 2nd ch away from hook (6 sts).

**Rnd 1:** (Inc, sc 2) 2 times (8 sts).

**Rnd 2:** (Inc, sc 3) 2 times (10 sts).

**Rnd 3:** (Inc, sc 4) 2 times (12 sts).

**Rnds 4–5:** Sc in each st (12 sts).

**Rnd 6:** Dec 6 times (6 sts).

Fasten off and leave a 6-inch (15-cm) tail for sewing. Do not stuff.

## Tail

With MC, ch 2 and inc 3 times in the 2nd ch away from hook (6 sts).

**Rnd 1:** Inc in each st (12 sts).

Fasten off and leave a 6-inch (15-cm) tail for sewing.

## Antlers (make 2)

With C2, ch 2 and inc 3 times in the 2nd ch away from hook (6 sts).

**Rnd 1:** Sc in each st (6 sts).

**Rnd 2:** Sc 5, Puff st (6 sts).

**Rnds 3–5:** Sc in each st (6 sts). Stuff the Antlers.

Fasten off and leave a 6-inch (15-cm) tail for sewing.

## Head

With C1, ch 2 and inc 3 times in the 2nd ch away from hook (6 sts).

**Rnd 1:** Inc 6 times (12 sts).

**Rnd 2:** With C1, sc 3. With MC sc 2. With C1, sc 7 (12 sts).

**Rnd 3:** With C1, inc in next 3 sts. With MC, sc 3. With C1, inc in next 3 sts, sc 3 (18 sts).

**Rnd 4:** With MC, inc. With C1, sc 2, inc, sc 2. With MC, inc, sc 2, inc. With C1, sc 2, inc, sc 2. With MC, inc, sc 2 (24 sts). If using safety eyes, attach them on this round, 12 sts apart.

**Rnd 5:** With MC, sc 3. With C1, sc 5. With MC, sc 7. With C1, sc 5. With MC, sc 4 (24 sts).

**Rnd 6:** With MC, inc, sc 3. With C1, inc, sc 3. With MC, (inc, sc 3) 2 times. With C1, inc, sc 3. With MC, inc, sc 3 (30 sts).

**Rnd 7:** With MC, sc 6. With C1, sc 4. With MC, sc 11. With C1, sc 4. With MC, sc 5 (30 sts). Break C1.

**Rnd 8:** With MC, (inc, sc 4) 6 times (36 sts).

**Rnds 9–11:** Sc in each st (36 sts).

**Rnd 12:** (Dec, sc 4) 6 times (30 sts).

**Rnd 13:** Sc in each st (30 sts). Stuff the Head.

**Rnd 14:** (Dec, sc 3) 6 times (24 sts).

**Rnd 15:** (Dec, sc 2) 6 times (18 sts).

**Rnd 16:** (Dec, sc) 6 times (12 sts).

**Rnd 17:** Dec 6 times (6 sts).

Fasten off and sew the hole closed.

## Assembly

Sew the Head to the top of the Body. Then, embroider a nose onto the face, covering Rnds 1–2 of the Head (see images 1–4 above). Sew each Antler onto Rnd 9 of the Head, 8 sts apart. Sew Rnd 6 of the Ears right below each Antler. Finally, sew the Tail to the back of the Body, on Rnd 10. Weave in all ends.

If you prefer to embroider the eyes instead of using safety eyes, set them 12 sts apart on Rnd 4 of the Head (for more information on sewing eyes onto plushies, see page 13).

# Wren the Wolf

In the wild, wolf packs are similar to human families. It would be so cute to make a wolf for each of your family members! This plush uses the typical gray hue, but feel free to use different colors to create your wolf.

## Skill Level
Intermediate

## Size
Approx 6 inches (15 cm) long, 4.5 inches (11.5 cm) wide and 10 inches (25.5 cm) tall

## Yarn
Super chunky chenille yarn, Premier Yarns Parfait Chunky, 100% polyester, 131 yds (120 m) and 3.5 oz (100 g) per skein

- Seal (MC), 2 skeins, 262 yds (240 m) total
- Cream (C1), ½ skein, approx 66 yds (60 m) total
- Black (C2), ⅓ skein, 44 yds (40 m) total

## Hooks
US size H-8 (5mm)

## Notions
Polyester fiberfill
Removable marker used to mark the first stitch of the round
Tapestry needle
Pair of 10mm safety eyes (optional)

## Gauge
20 sc x 5 rounds = 4 inches (10 cm)

### Abbreviations

**C1** = color 1

**C2** = color 2

**Ch(s)** = chain(s)

**Dec** = decrease (crochet 2 sc together)

**Flo** = front loop only

**Inc** = increase (work 2 sc into one stitch)

**MC** = main color

**Sc** = single crochet

**Sl st** = slip stitch

**St(s)** = stitch(es)

## Legs (make 4)

With C1, ch 2 and inc 3 times in the 2nd ch away from hook (6 sts).

**Rnd 1:** Inc in each st (12 sts).

**Rnds 2–6:** Sc in each st (12 sts).

Fasten off and leave a 3-inch (7.5-cm) tail. Do not stuff.

## Tail

With C1, ch 2 and inc 3 times in the 2nd ch away from hook (6 sts).

**Rnd 1:** Inc 6 times (12 sts).

**Rnds 2–6:** Sc in each st (12 sts). Break C1.

**Rnds 7–10:** With MC, sc in each st (12 sts).

**Rnd 11:** (Dec, sc) 4 times (8 sts). Only stuff Rnds 1–8.

**Rnd 12:** Sc in each st (8 sts).

**Rnd 13:** Ch 1. Fold the Tail in half side to side, and sc across through both sides (for more information on sc across both sides, see Gale the Giraffe, page 59).

Fasten off and leave a 3-inch (7.5-cm) tail.

## Ears (make 2)

With MC, ch 2 and inc 2 times in the 2nd ch away from hook (4 sts).

**Rnd 1:** Sc in each st (4 sts).

**Rnd 2:** With MC, inc. With C1, sc. with MC, inc, sc (6 sts).

**Rnd 3:** With MC, inc, sc. With C1, sc, inc. With MC, sc 2 (8 sts).

**Rnd 4:** With MC, inc, sc 2. With C1, sc, inc, sc 2. With MC, sc (10 sts).

**Rnd 5:** Ch 1. Fold the Ear in half side to side, and sc across through both sides (for more information on sc across both sides, see Gale the Giraffe, page 59).

Fasten off and leave a 3-inch (7.5-cm) tail. Do not stuff.

## Body

With C1, ch 10. Inc in the 2nd ch from hook, sc in the next 7 chs, and inc 2 times in the last ch. Turn your work clockwise 180 degrees, so that you can work along the opposite side of the ch. Then sc in the next 7 chs, and inc in the last ch (22 sts).

**Rnd 1:** Inc in the next 2 sts, sc 7, inc in the next 4 sts, sc 7, inc in the last 2 sts (30 sts).

**Rnd 2:** (Sc 2, attach Leg with 3 sts, sc 5, attach the next Leg with 3 sts, sc 2) 2 times (30 sts) (for more information on attaching legs, see page 10).

**Rnd 3:** With C1, sc in the next 2 sts of the Body. With MC, sc in the remaining 9 sts of the next Leg. With C1, sc in the next 5 sts of the Body. With MC, sc in the remaining 9 sts of the next Leg. With C1, sc in the next 4 sts of the Body. With MC, sc in the remaining 9 sts of the next Leg. With C1, sc in the next 5 sts of the Body. In the remaining 9 sts of the Leg, with MC, sc 7. With C1, sc 2. Sc in the remaining 2 sts of the Body (54 sts).

**Rnd 4:** With C1, sc 3. With MC, sc 9. With C1, sc 4. With MC, sc 10. With C1, sc 3. With MC, sc 10. With C1, sc 4. With MC, sc 7. With C1, sc 4 (54 sts).

**Rnd 5:** With C1, sc 4. With MC, sc 46. With C1, sc 4 (54 sts).

**Rnds 6–7:** With C1, sc 4. With MC, sc 47. With C1, sc 3 (54 sts).

**Rnd 8:** With C1, sc 5. With MC, sc 46. With C1, sc 3 (54 sts).

**Rnd 9:** With C1, sc 5. With MC, sc 47. With C1, sc 2 (54 sts).

**Rnd 10:** With C1, sc 5. With MC, sc 48. With C1, sc (54 sts).

**Rnd 11:** With C1, sc 5. With MC, sc 49 (54 sts). Break C1.

**Rnd 12:** With MC, sc in each st (54 sts).

**Rnd 13:** With MC, sc 16, (dec, sc 3) 6 times, sc 8 (48 sts). Stuff lightly as you work.

**Rnd 14:** Sc in each st (48 sts).

**Rnd 15:** Sc 16, (dec, sc 2) 6 times, sc 8 (42 sts).

**Rnd 16:** Sc in each st (42 sts).

**Rnd 17:** Sc 16, (dec, sc) 6 times, sc 8 (36 sts).

**Rnd 18:** Sc 21. Place your hook into the flo of the 23rd and 22nd st (3 sts on hook). Sl st the sts together. Repeat this for the 24th and 21st st, the 25th and 20th st, the 26th and 19th st, the 27th and 18th st, the 28th and 17th st, the 29th and 16th st, the 30th and 15th st, the 31st and 14th st, and the 32nd and 13th st (for more information on closing off a body, see Flynn the Fox, page 29). Sc in the 33rd st, and the remaining 3 sts of this Rnd and the first 12 sts of the next Rnd. This is the new beginning of the Rnd (16 sts). Stuff the Body. Overstuff the Body on Rnds 16–18.

**Rnds 19–22:** Sc in each st (16 sts). This is the Neck portion.

Fasten off and leave a 6-inch (15-cm) tail for sewing. Finish stuffing the Body and Neck.

## Head

With C1, ch 2 and inc 3 times in the 2nd ch away from hook (6 sts).

**Rnd 1:** With C1, inc. With MC, inc 2 times. With C1, inc 3 times (12 sts).

**Rnd 2:** With C1, (sc, inc) 2 times. With MC, (sc, inc) 2 times. With C1, (sc, inc) 2 times (18 sts).

**Rnd 3:** With C1, sc 4. With MC, sc 5. With C1, sc 9 (18 sts).

**Rnd 4:** With C1, sc 5. With MC, sc 4. With C1, sc 9 (18 sts).

**Rnd 5:** With C1, sc 5, inc in the flo. With MC, inc 3 times. With C1, inc, sc 8 (23 sts).

**Rnd 6:** With C1, sc 5, inc, sc. With MC, (inc, sc) 3 times, sc. With C1, sc again into the last st. (You should have an increase with one sc in MC and the other in C1.) With C1, sc 9 (28 sts). If using safety eyes, attach them on this round, 14 sts apart.

**Rnd 7:** With C1, sc 8. With MC, sc 11. With C1, sc 9 (28 sts).

**Rnd 8:** With C1, sc 7. With MC, sc 14. With C1, sc 7 (28 sts).

**Rnd 9:** With C1, sc 6. With MC, sc 17. With C1, sc 5 (28 sts).

**Rnd 10:** With C1, sc 5. With MC, sc 21. With C1, sc 2 (28 sts).

**Rnd 11:** With C1, sc 5. With MC, sc 4. Attach Ear with 5 sts, sc 2, attach Ear with 5 sts, sc 4. With C1, sc 3 (28 sts).

**Rnd 12:** With C1, sc 3. With MC, sc 24. With C1, sc (28 sts).

**Rnd 13:** With C1, sc 3. With MC, sc 25 (28 sts). Break C1.

**Rnd 14:** With MC, sc in each st (28 sts).

**Rnd 15:** (Dec, sc 2) 7 times (21 sts). Stuff the Head.

**Rnd 16:** Sc in each st (21 sts).

**Rnd 17:** (Dec, sc) 7 times (14 sts).

**Rnd 18:** Dec 7 times (7 sts).

Fasten off and sew the hole closed.

## Assembly

Sew the Head to the top of the Body. When aligning it to the Neck, be sure to sew Rnds 7–12 of the Head to the Neck. Embroider a triangle-shaped nose with C2 onto the face, covering Rnds 1–2 of the Head (see images 1–4 above). Sew the Tail to the back of the Body, approximately at Rnd 14. Weave in all ends.

If you prefer to embroider the eyes instead of using safety eyes, set them 14 sts apart on Rnd 6 of the Head (for more information on sewing eyes onto plushies, see page 13).

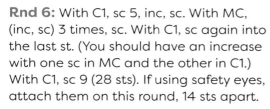

# Mia the Moose

Moose are huge, growing up to 10 feet (3 m) tall! Although their size is intimidating, this cuddle-size version will convey the opposite feeling. This moose is beginner friendly, and perfect for those who dislike the tedious work of color changing between stitches.

**Skill Level**
Beginner

**Size**
Approx 16 inches (40.5 cm) long, 8 inches (20.5 cm) wide and 10 inches (25.5 cm) tall

**Yarn**
Super chunky chenille yarn, Premier Yarns Parfait Chunky, 100% polyester, 131 yds (120 m) and 3.5 oz (100 g) per skein

- Teddy Bear (MC), 2 skeins, 262 yds (240 m) total

- Chocolate (C1), ½ skein, approx 66 yds (60 m) total

**Hooks**
US size H-8 (5mm)

**Notions**
Polyester fiberfill
Removable marker used to mark the first stitch of the round
Tapestry needle
Pair of 10mm safety eyes (optional)

**Gauge**
10 sc x 5 rounds = 4 inches (10 cm)

## Abbreviations

**Blo** = back loop only

**C1** = color 1

**Ch(s)** = chain(s)

**Dec** = decrease (crochet 2 sc together)

**Flo** = front loop only

**Inc** = increase (work 2 sc into one stitch)

**MC** = main color

**Sc** = single crochet

**Sl st** = slip stitch

**St(s)** = stitch(es)

## Pattern Stitches

**Puff Stitch** = Yarn over, insert your hook through the st, yarn over and then draw up a loop. Repeat until you have 6 loops on the hook. Yarn over and draw through all 6 loops.

## Legs (make 4)

With C1, ch 2 and inc 3 times in the 2nd ch away from hook (6 sts).

**Rnd 1:** Inc in each st (12 sts).

**Rnd 2:** Sc in the blo of each st (12 sts).

**Rnds 3-6:** With MC, sc in each st (12 sts).

Fasten off and leave a 6-inch (15-cm) tail for sewing.

## Tail

With MC, ch 6. Puff st in the 2nd ch from hook and sc in the remaining 4 chs. Fasten off and leave a 6-inch (15-cm) tail.

## Ears (make 2)

With MC, ch 2 and inc 3 times in the 2nd ch away from hook (6 sts).

**Rnd 1:** Sc in each st (6 sts).

**Rnd 2:** Inc 6 times (12 sts).

**Rnd 3:** (Inc, sc) 6 times (18 sts).

Fasten off and leave a 6-inch (15-cm) tail for sewing.

## Head

With MC, ch 2 and inc 3 times in the 2nd ch away from hook (6 sts).

**Rnd 1:** Inc 6 times (12 sts).

**Rnd 2:** (Inc, sc) 6 times (18 sts).

**Rnd 3:** (Inc, sc 2) 6 times (24 sts).

**Rnd 4:** Sc 8, Puff st, sc 5, Puff st, sc 9 (24 sts).

**Rnd 5:** (Inc, sc 3) 6 times (30 sts).

**Rnds 6-8:** Sc in each st (30 sts).

**Rnd 9:** (Dec, sc 3) 6 times (24 sts).

**Rnd 10:** Sc in each st (24 sts).

**Rnd 11:** (Dec, sc 2) 6 times (18 sts).

**Rnd 12:** In the flo, (inc, sc 2) 6 times (24 sts). If using safety eyes, attach them 11 sts apart on this Rnd.

**Rnd 13:** (Inc, sc 3) 6 times (30 sts).

**Rnds 14-16:** Sc in each st (30 sts).

**Rnd 17:** (Dec, sc 3) 6 times (24 sts).

**Rnd 18:** (Dec, sc 2) 6 times (18 sts).

**Rnd 19:** (Dec, sc) 6 times (12 sts).

**Rnd 20:** Dec 6 times (6 sts).

Fasten off and leave an 8-inch (20.5-cm) tail. Sew the hole closed.

## Body

With MC, ch 13. Inc in the 2nd ch from hook, sc in the next 10 chs, and inc 2 times in the last ch. Turn your work clockwise 180 degrees, so that you can work along the opposite side of the ch. Then sc in the next 10 chs, and inc in the last ch (28 sts).

**Rnd 1:** Inc in the first 2 sts, sc 10, inc 4 times, sc 10, inc 2 times (36 sts).

**Rnd 2:** (Sc 2, attach Leg with 3 sts, sc 8, attach the next Leg with 3 sts, sc 2) 2 times (36 sts) (for more information on attaching legs, see page 10).

**Rnd 3:** (Sc in the next 2 sts of the Body, sc in the remaining 9 sts of the next Leg, sc in the next 8 sts of the Body, sc in the remaining 9 sts of the next Leg, sc in the next 2 sts of the Body) 2 times (60 sts).

**Rnds 4–12:** Sc in each st (60 sts).

**Rnd 13:** (Dec, sc 8) 6 times (54 sts).

**Rnds 14–15:** Sc in each st (54 sts).

**Rnd 16:** (Dec, sc 7) 6 times (48 sts).

**Rnd 17:** (Dec, sc 6) 6 times (42 sts).

**Rnd 18:** Sc 13, (dec, sc 2) 6 times, sc 5 (36 sts). Stuff lightly as you work.

**Rnd 19:** Sc 13, (dec, sc) 6 times, sc 5 (30 sts).

**Rnd 20:** Sc 13, dec 6, sc 5 (24 sts).

**Rnd 21:** Sc 15. Place your hook into the flo of the 16th and 17th st (3 sts on hook). Sl st the sts together. Repeat this for the 18th and 15th st, and the 19th and 14th st (for more information on closing off a body, see Flynn the Fox, page 29). Sc in the 20th st and the remaining 17 sts that were left untouched. This is the new beginning of the Rnd (18 sts). Stuff the Body. Overstuff the Body on Rnds 18–21.

**Rnds 22–23:** Sc in each st (18 sts). This is the Neck portion.

Fasten off and leave a 6-inch (15-cm) tail for sewing.

## Antler Buds (make 2)

In C1, ch 2 and inc 3 times in the 2nd ch away from hook (6 sts).

**Rnds 1–3:** Sc in each st (6 sts).

Fasten off and leave a 6-inch (15-cm) tail for sewing.

**Rnd 6:** Sc 4, attach Antler Bud with 2 sts (6 sts).

**Rnd 7:** Sc in the first 4 sts of the Antler, sc in the remaining 4 sts of the Antler Bud (8 sts).

**Rnd 8:** (Dec, sc 2) 2 times (6 sts). Stuff the Antler.

**Rnds 9–13:** Sc in each st (6 sts).

Fasten off and leave a 6-inch (15-cm) tail for sewing.

## Assembly

Sew the Head to the Neck portion of the Body. Sew the Ears to Rnd 16 of the Head, 8 sts apart. Make sure that the Puff sts on Rnd 4 of the Head are about 1 inch (2.5 cm) away from each Ear. Sew the Antlers on Rnd 16 of the Head, on the side of each Ear. Finally, sew the Tail to the back of the Body, on Rnd 14. Weave in all ends.

If you prefer to embroider the eyes instead of using safety eyes, set them 10 sts apart on Rnd 12 of the Head (for more information on sewing eyes onto plushies, see page 13).

## Antlers (make 2)

In C1, ch 2 and inc 3 times in the 2nd ch away from hook (6 sts).

**Rnds 1–2:** Sc in each st (6 sts).

**Rnds 3–5:** Dec 2 times, inc 2 times (6 sts).

# Lily the Ladybug

Such a tiny bug, but the plushie size is the opposite! Instead of watching a ladybug crawl on your finger, you'll be able to hold one between your hands! This pattern is unique because you create two bowl-shaped pieces for the wings and join them to a ball-shaped body piece!

## Skill Level
Intermediate

## Size
Approx 7 inches (18 cm) long, 6 inches (15 cm) wide and 8 inches (20.5 cm) tall

## Yarn
Super chunky chenille yarn, Premier Yarns Parfait Chunky, 100% polyester, 131 yds (120 m) and 3.5 oz (100 g) per skein

- Cardinal (MC), 2 skeins, 262 yds (240 m) total
- Black (C1), ½ skein, approx 66 yds (60 m) total
- Seashell (C2), ½ skein, approx 66 yds (60 m) total

## Hooks
US size H-8 (5mm)

## Notions
Polyester fiberfill
Removable marker used to mark the first stitch of the round
Tapestry needle
Pair of 6mm safety eyes (optional)

## Gauge
10 sc x 5 rounds = 4 inches (10 cm)

### Abbreviations
**C1** = color 1
**C2** = color 2
**Ch(s)** = chain(s)
**Dec** = decrease (crochet 2 sc together)
**Flo** = front loop only
**Inc** = increase (work 2 sc into one stitch)
**MC** = main color
**Sc** = single crochet
**Sl st** = slip stitch
**St(s)** = stitch(es)

### Pattern Stitches
**Puff Stitch** = Yarn over, insert your hook through the st, yarn over and then draw up a loop. Repeat until you have 6 loops on the hook. Yarn over and draw through all 6 loops.

## Legs (make 6)

With C1, ch 7. Puff st in the 2nd ch from hook. Sc in the remaining 5 sts (6 sts).

Fasten off and leave a 3-inch (7.5-cm) tail for sewing. Do not stuff.

## Antennae (make 2)

With C1, ch 7. Puff st in the 2nd ch from hook. Sl st in the remaining 5 sts (6 sts).

Fasten off and leave a 6-inch (15-cm) tail for sewing.

## Wings (make 2)

With MC, ch 2 and inc 3 times in the 2nd ch away from hook (6 sts).

**Rnd 1:** Inc 6 times (12 sts).

**Rnd 2:** (Inc, sc) 6 times (18 sts).

**Rnd 3:** With MC, (inc, sc 2) 2 times, inc. With C1, sc 2. With MC, (inc, sc 2) 3 times (24 sts).

**Rnd 4:** With MC, (inc, sc 3) 2 times, inc, sc. With C1, sc 2, inc. With MC, sc 3, (inc, sc 3) 2 times (30 sts).

**Rnd 5:** With MC, (inc, sc 4) 2 times, inc, sc 3. With C1, sc, inc, sc. With MC, sc 3, (inc, sc 4) 2 times (36 sts).

**Rnd 6:** With MC, sc 26. With C1, sc 2. With MC, sc 8 (36 sts).

**Rnd 7:** With MC, sc 26. With C1, sc 3. With MC, sc 7 (36 sts).

**Rnd 8:** With MC, sc 27. With C1, sc 2. With MC, sc 7 (36 sts).

**Rnd 9:** With MC, sc 32. With C1, sc 2. With MC, sc 2 (36 sts).

**Rnd 10:** With MC, sc 19. With C1, sc 2. With MC, sc 11. With C1, sc 3. With MC, sc (36 sts).

**Rnd 11:** With MC, sc 19. With C1, sc 3. With MC, sc 11. With C1, sc 2. With MC, sc (36 sts).

**Rnd 12:** With MC, sc 20. With C1, sc 2. With MC, sc 14 (36 sts).

**Rnd 13:** With MC, (dec, sc 4) 6 times (30 sts).

**Rnd 14:** With MC, sc 20. With C1, sc 2. With MC, sc 8 (30 sts).

**Rnd 15:** With MC, sc 20. With C1, sc 3. With MC, sc 4. With C1, sc 2. With MC, sc (30 sts).

**Rnd 16:** With MC, sc 21. With C1, sc 2. With MC, sc 4. With C1, sc 3 (30 sts).

**Rnd 17:** With MC, sc 28. With C1, sc 2 (30 sts).

**Rnd 18:** With MC, (dec, sc 3) 6 times (24 sts).

**Rnd 19:** With MC, (dec, sc 2) 3 times, dec. With C1, sc 2. With MC, (dec, sc 2) 2 times (18 sts).

**Rnd 20:** With MC, sc 10. With C1, sc 3. With MC, sc 5 (18 sts). Cut off C1. Do not stuff the Wing.

**Rnd 21:** Sc 9. Ch 1. Fold the Wing in half side to side and sc across both sides (9 sts) (for more information on sc across both sides, see Gale the Giraffe, page 59).

Fold the Wing flat so that the side without spots is concave. You should have a bowl-like shape, with the spots on the outside of the bowl.

Fasten off and leave a 6-inch (18-cm) tail.

## Head and Body

With C1, ch 2 and inc 3 times in the 2nd ch away from hook (6 sts).

**Rnd 1:** Inc 6 times (12 sts).

**Rnd 2:** (Inc, sc) 6 times (18 sts).

**Rnd 3:** (Inc, sc 2) 6 times (24 sts).

**Rnd 4:** (Inc, sc 3) 6 times (30 sts).

**Rnd 5:** (Inc, sc 4) 6 times (36 sts).

**Rnd 6:** (Inc, sc 5) 6 times (42 sts).

**Rnd 7:** (Inc, sc 6) 6 times (48 sts).

**Rnds 8–13:** Sc in each st (48 sts).

**Rnd 14:** (Dec, sc 6) 6 times (42 sts).

**Rnds 15–17:** Sc in each st (42 sts).

**Rnd 18:** (Dec, sc 5) 6 times (36 sts).

**Rnds 19–20:** Sc in each st (36 sts).

**Rnd 21:** (Dec, sc 4) 6 times (30 sts).

**Rnd 22:** Sc in each st (30 sts).

**Rnd 23:** (Dec, sc 3) 6 times (24 sts).

**Rnd 24:** Sc 4. Attach the Wing to the Body with 8 sts, attach the next Wing to the Body with 8 sts, sc 4 (24 sts) (for more information on attaching limbs, see page 10). Stuff the Body. Break C1.

**Rnd 25:** With C2, sc in the flo of each st (24 sts).

**Rnd 26:** Sc in each st (24 sts).

**Rnd 27:** Sc 12. Attach the first Antenna by placing your hook into the last st on the Antenna and the next st of the Body. Sc the sts together. Sc 1. Attach the 2nd Antenna in the same way as the first Antenna. Sc 9 (24 sts).

**Rnds 28–29:** Sc in each st (24 sts). If using safety eyes, attach them on Rnd 28, 11 sts apart.

**Rnd 30:** (Dec, sc 2) 6 times (18 sts).

**Rnd 31:** (Dec, sc) 6 times (12 sts). Stuff the Head.

**Rnd 32:** Dec 6 times (6 sts).

Fasten off and sew the hole closed.

## Assembly

Sew each Leg onto Body one Rnd apart, starting from Rnd 14 to Rnd 19, about 1.5 inches (4 cm) under each Wing. Weave in all ends.

If you prefer to embroider the eyes instead of using safety eyes, set them on Rnd 28 11 sts apart. You can also sew Rnd 1 of each Wing to Rnd 7 of the Body to keep the Wings in place if you'd like.

# Joyful Jungle

Welcome to the captivating realm of the jungle! Vibrant life exists in every corner. Amidst the lush foliage and echoing calls, colorful animals roam freely. From the mighty rhino to the graceful sloth, this untamed world teems with awe-inspiring wildlife. As you immerse yourself in this exotic kingdom, be sure to grab as many vibrant colors as you can! Crocheting the animals of the jungle allows you to capture their essence with each carefully crafted stitch.

The animals in this chapter are wild and very vibrant in color! You can bring the charm and allure of these incredible creatures into your own home, and experience the joy and fulfillment that comes with bringing your newfound crochet creations to life. Some of these animals require a bit of sewing. But luckily, only a handful of body parts are truly necessary to be sewn together to create the final plushie.

# Sid the Sloth

Sloths may be slow, but Sid works up quite fast! This sloth pattern only requires two pieces to be sewn together at the end of the completed crocheted pieces—so if you're not a fan of sewing, here's another minimal sewing pattern!

## Skill Level
Intermediate

## Size
Approx 8 inches (20.5 cm) long, 9 inches (23 cm) wide and 16 inches (41 cm) tall

## Yarn
Super chunky chenille yarn, Premier Yarns Parfait Chunky, 100% polyester, 131 yds (120 m) and 3.5 oz (100 g) per skein

- Toffee (MC), 2 skeins, 262 yds (240 m) total
- Cream (C1), ½ skein, approx 66 yds (60 m) total
- Teddy Bear (C2), ½ skein, approx 66 yds (60 m) total

## Hooks
US size H-8 (5mm)

## Notions
Polyester fiberfill
Removable marker used to mark the first stitch of the round
Tapestry needle
Pair of 6mm safety eyes (optional)

## Gauge
10 sc x 5 rounds = 4 inches (10 cm)

### Abbreviations
C1 = color 1
C2 = color 2
Ch(s) = chain(s)
Dec = decrease (crochet 2 sc together)
Flo = front loop only
Inc = increase (work 2 sc into one stitch)
MC = main color
Sc = single crochet
St(s) = stitch(es)

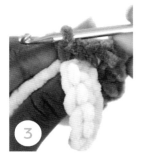

## Legs (make 2)

With MC, ch 2 and inc 3 times in the 2nd ch away from hook (6 sts).

**Rnd 1:** Inc in each st (12 sts).

**Rnd 2:** With MC, sc, inc in the next 2 sts. With C1, (ch 6, sc in the 2nd ch from hook, and the remaining 4 chs. Sc in the next st) 3 times. These are the sloth's three claws! With MC, inc in the next 2 sts, sc 4 (16 sts).

**Rnd 3:** With MC, sc in each st (16 sts) (images 1–4). When working around the claws in this row, make sure that the claws are in front of the hook when you work into the next st to allow them to lie flat.

**Note:** While the sloth in images 1–4 is brown, yours will be gray.

**Rnds 4–11:** Sc in each st (16 sts).

**Rnd 12:** (Dec, sc 2) 4 times (12 sts).

**Rnds 13–15:** Sc in each st (12 sts).

**Rnd 16:** (Dec, sc) 4 times (8 sts).

**Rnd 17:** Sc in each st (8 sts).

**Rnd 18:** Sc 2, ch 1. Fold the Leg in half from side to side, and sc across through both sides (4 sts) (for more information on sc across both sides, see Gale the Giraffe, page 59).

Fasten off and leave a 6-inch (15-cm) tail.

## Arms (make 2)

With MC, ch 2 and inc 3 times in the 2nd ch away from hook (6 sts).

**Rnd 1:** Inc in each st (12 sts).

**Rnd 2:** With MC, sc 3. With C1, (ch 6, sc in the 2nd ch from hook, and the remaining 4 chs. Sc in the next st) 3 times. With MC, sc 5 (16 sts).

**Rnd 3:** With MC, sc in each st (12 sts).

**Rnds 4–15:** Sc in each st (12 sts).

**Rnd 16:** (Dec, sc) 4 times (8 sts).

**Rnds 17–24:** Sc in each st (8 sts).

**Rnd 25:** Sc, ch 1. Fold the Arm in half from side to side, and sc across through both sides (4 sts) (for more information on sc across both sides, see Gale the Giraffe, page 59).

Fasten off and leave a 6-inch (15-cm) tail.

## Body

With MC, ch 2 and inc 3 times in the 2nd ch away from hook (6 sts).

**Rnd 1:** Inc in each st (12 sts).

**Rnd 2:** (Inc, sc) 6 times (18 sts).

**Rnd 3:** (Inc, sc 2) 6 times (24 sts).

**Rnd 4:** (Inc, sc 3) 6 times (30 sts).

**Rnd 5:** (Inc, sc 4) 6 times (36 sts).

**Rnd 6:** (Inc, sc 5) 6 times (42 sts).

**Rnd 7:** Sc 6. Attach Leg 1 with 4 sts, making sure the toes of the Leg face you. Sc 13. Attach Leg 2 with 4 sts. Sc 15 (42 sts). Stuff lightly as you work.

**Rnds 8–13:** Sc in each st (42 sts).

**Rnd 14:** (Dec, sc 5) 6 times (36 sts).

**Rnds 15–17:** Sc in each st (36 sts).

**Rnd 18:** (Dec, sc 4) 6 times (30 sts).

**Rnds 19–22:** Sc in each st (30 sts).

**Rnd 23:** (Dec, sc 3) 6 times (24 sts).

**Rnds 24–25:** Sc in each st (24 sts). Stuff the Body.

**Rnd 26:** (Dec, sc 2) 6 times (18 sts).

**Rnd 27:** Sc 4. Attach Arm 1 with 4 sts. Sc 5. Attach Arm 2 with 4 sts. Sc (18 sts).

Fasten off and leave a 6-inch (15-cm) tail. Finish stuffing the Body.

## Head

With C1, ch 2 and inc 3 times in the 2nd ch away from hook (6 sts).

**Rnd 1:** Inc 6 times (12 sts).

**Rnd 2:** Sc in each st (12 sts).

**Rnd 3:** Sc 3, inc in the flo of the next 6 sts, sc 3 (18 sts).

**Rnd 4:** With C1, inc, sc 2, inc. With C2, sc 2. With C1, inc, sc 2, inc. With C2, sc 2. With C1, (inc, sc 2) 2 times (24 sts).

**Rnd 5:** With C1, inc, sc 3, inc. With C2, sc 3, inc. With C1, sc 2. With MC, sc. With C1, inc, sc. With C2, sc 2, inc, sc. With C1, sc 2, inc, sc 3 (30 sts).

**Rnd 6:** With C1, inc, sc 4, inc. With C2, sc 4, inc, sc. With MC, sc 3, inc, sc 2. With C2, sc 2, inc, sc 3. With MC, sc, inc, sc 4 (36 sts). Break C1.

**Rnd 7:** With MC, sc 8. With C2, sc 6. With MC, sc 9. With C2, sc 7. With MC, sc 6 (36 sts).

**Rnd 8:** With MC, sc 9. With C2, sc 4. With MC, sc 12. With C2, sc 5. With MC, sc 6 (36 sts). Break C2.

**Rnds 9–10:** With MC, sc in each st (36 sts).

**Rnd 11:** (Dec, sc 4) 6 times (30 sts).

**Rnd 12:** Sc in each st (30 sts).

**Rnd 13:** (Dec, sc 3) 6 times (24 sts).

**Rnd 14:** (Dec, sc 2) 6 times (18 sts). Stuff the Head.

**Rnd 15:** (Dec, sc) 6 times (12 sts).

**Rnd 16:** Dec 6 times (6 sts).

Fasten off and sew the hole closed.

## Assembly

Sew the Head to the top of the Body. Then embroider a nose onto the face, covering Rnds 1–2 of the Head (see images 5–8 above). Weave in all ends.

**Optional:** If you prefer to embroider the eyes instead of using safety eyes, set them 10 sts apart on Rnd 5 of the Head (for more information on sewing eyes onto plushies, see page 13).

# Gale the Giraffe

Giraffes are the tallest mammals in the world! They love to hang out in groups, so you might need to make several of these plushies so your giraffe doesn't get lonely. Because the neck and body are crocheted together, add extra stuffing to the base of the neck for extra support.

## Skill Level
Intermediate

## Size
Approx 16 inches (40.5 cm) long, 8 inches (20.5 cm) wide and 14 inches (35.5 cm) tall

## Yarn
Super chunky chenille yarn, Premier Yarns Parfait Chunky, 100% polyester, 131 yds (120 m) and 3.5 oz (100 g) per skein

- Sunshine (MC), 2 skeins, 262 yds (240 m) total
- Teddy Bear (C1), ½ skein, approx 66 yds (60 m) total
- Toffee (C2), ½ skein, approx 66 yds (60 m) total

## Hooks
US size H-8 (5mm)

## Notions
Polyester fiberfill
Removable marker used to mark the first stitch of the round
Tapestry needle
Pair of 10mm safety eyes (optional)

## Gauge
10 sc x 5 rounds = 4 inches (10 cm)

### Abbreviations
**Blo** = back loop only
**C1** = color 1
**C2** = color 2
**Ch(s)** = chain(s)
**Dec** = decrease (crochet 2 sc together)
**Flo** = front loop only
**Inc** = increase (work 2 sc into one stitch)
**MC** = main color
**Sc** = single crochet
**Sl st** = slip stitch
**St(s)** = stitch(es)

### Pattern Stitches
**Puff Stitch** = Yarn over, insert your hook through the st, yarn over and then draw up a loop. Repeat until you have 6 loops on the hook. Yarn over and draw through all 6 loops.

## Legs (make 4)

With C1, ch 2 and inc 3 times in the 2nd ch away from hook (6 sts).

**Rnd 1:** Inc in each st (12 sts).

**Rnd 2:** Sc in the blo of each st (12 sts).

**Rnds 3–7:** With MC, sc in each st (12 sts).

Fasten off and leave a 6-inch (15-cm) tail for sewing.

## Tail

With MC, ch 6. With C1, Puff st in the 2nd ch from hook. Break C1. With MC, sc in the remaining 4 chs. Fasten off and leave a 6-inch (15-cm) tail.

## Ears (make 2)

With MC, ch 2 and inc 3 times in the 2nd ch away from hook (6 sts).

**Rnd 1:** Sc in each st (6 sts).

**Rnd 2:** Inc 6 times (12 sts).

Fasten off and leave a 6-inch (15-cm) tail for sewing.

## Head

With C2, ch 2 and inc 3 times in the 2nd ch away from hook (6 sts).

**Rnd 1:** Inc 6 times (12 sts).

**Rnd 2:** (Inc, sc) 6 times (18 sts).

**Rnds 3–5:** Sc in each st (18 sts). Break C2.

**Rnd 6:** With MC, (inc, sc 2) 6 times (24 sts).

**Rnd 7:** (Inc, sc 3) 6 times (30 sts).

**Rnds 8–11:** Sc in each st (30 sts). Add safety eyes 15 sts apart on Rnd 9 after completing Rnd 2 of the Body.

Fasten off and leave a 6-inch (15-cm) tail.

## Body

With MC, ch 13. Inc in the 2nd ch from hook, sc in the next 10 chs, and inc 2 times in the last ch. Turn your work clockwise 180 degrees, so that you can work along the opposite side of the ch. Then sc in the next 10 chs, and inc in the last ch (28 sts).

**Rnd 1:** Inc in the first 2 sts, sc 10, inc in the next 4 sts, sc 10, inc in the last 2 sts (36 sts).

**Rnd 2:** (Sc 2, attach Leg with 3 sts, sc 8, attach the next Leg with 3 sts, sc 2) 2 times (36 sts) (for more information on attaching legs, see page 10).

**Rnd 3:** (Sc in the next 2 sts of the Body, sc in the remaining 9 sts of the next Leg, sc in the next 8 sts of the Body, sc in the remaining 9 sts of the next Leg, sc in the next 2 sts of the Body) 2 times (60 sts).

**Rnds 4–6:** Sc in each st (60 sts).

**Rnd 7:** With MC, sc 51, With C1, sc 2. With MC, sc 7 (60 sts).

**Rnd 8:** With MC, sc 51, With C1, sc 3. With MC, sc 6 (60 sts).

**Rnd 9:** With MC, sc 16. With C1, sc 2. With MC, sc 34. With C1, sc 2. With MC, sc 6 (60 sts).

**Rnd 10:** With MC, sc 16. With C1, sc 3. With MC, sc 26. With C1, sc 2. With MC, sc 13 (60 sts).

**Rnd 11:** With MC, sc 17. With C1, sc 2. With MC, sc 26. With C1, sc 3. With MC, sc 12 (60 sts).

**Rnd 12:** With MC, sc 11. With C1, sc 2. With MC, sc 33. With C1, sc 2. With MC, sc 12 (60 sts).

**Rnd 13:** With MC, dec, sc 8. With C2, dec, sc 2. With MC, sc 6, dec, (sc 8, dec) 3 times, sc 4. With C2, sc 2. With MC, sc 2 (54 sts).

**Rnd 14:** With MC, sc 10. With C1, sc 2. With MC, sc 11. With C1, sc 2. With MC, sc 12. With C1, sc 2. With MC, sc 11. With C1, sc 3. With MC, sc (54 sts).

**Rnd 15:** With MC, sc 23. With C1, sc 3. With MC, sc 11. With C1, sc 3. With MC, sc 11. With C1, sc 2. With MC, sc (54 sts).

**Rnd 16:** With MC, (dec, sc 7) 2 times, dec, sc 4. With C1, sc 2. With MC, sc, dec, sc 7, dec. With C1, sc 2. With MC, sc 5, dec, sc 7 (48 sts). Break C1.

**Rnd 17:** (Dec, sc 6) 6 times (42 sts).

**Rnd 18:** Sc 13, (dec, sc 2) 6 times, sc 5 (36 sts). Stuff lightly as you work.

**Rnd 19:** Sc 13, (dec, sc) 6 times, sc 5 (30 sts).

**Rnd 20:** Sc 13, dec 6 times, sc 5 (24 sts).

**Rnd 21:** Sc 15. Place your hook into the flo of the 16th and 17th st (3 sts on hook). Sl st the sts together. Repeat this for the 18th and 15th st, the 19th and 14th st, the 20th and 13th st, the 21st and the 12th st (for more information on closing off a body, see Flynn the Fox, page 29). Inc in the 22nd st, and sc in the remaining 2 sts of this Rnd and the first 11 sts of the next Rnd (15 sts). This is the new beginning of the Rnd (15 sts). Stuff the Body. Over-stuff the Body on Rnds 18–21.

**Rnds 22–24:** Sc in each st (15 sts). This is the Neck portion.

**Rnd 25:** Sc 6, attach the Head with 6 sts, sc 3 (15 sts) (for more information on attaching legs, see page 10).

**Rnd 26:** Sc in the next 6 sts of the Neck. Sc in the remaining 24 sts of the Head. Sc in the remaining 3 sts of the Neck (33 sts).

**Rnd 27:** Sc 4, dec 2 times, sc 20, dec 2 times, sc (29 sts). If using safety eyes, attach them on this round, to Rnd 9 of the Head 15 sts apart.

**Rnd 28:** Sc in each st (29 sts).

**Rnd 29:** Sc 3, dec 2 times, sc 18, dec 2 times (25 sts).

**Rnd 30:** Sc in each st (25 sts). Stuff the Head and Neck.

**Rnd 31:** (Dec, sc 3) 5 times (20 sts).

**Rnd 32:** (Dec, sc 2) 5 times (15 sts).

**Rnd 33:** (Dec, sc) 5 times (10 sts).

**Rnd 34:** Dec 5 times (5 sts).

Fasten off and sew the hole closed.

## Mane Piece (make 5)

With C1, ch 2 and inc 3 times in the 2nd ch away from hook (6 sts).

**Rnd 1:** (Sc 2, inc) 2 times (8 sts).

**Rnd 2:** Sc in each st (8 sts).

Fasten off the first 4 Mane pieces and leave a 3-inch (7.5-cm) tail. Do not fasten off the 5th Mane Piece. Instead, Ch 1, fold the piece in half, and sc across both sides (see images 1–2 above).

Then (fold one Mane Piece in half, place your hook into the 1st and 8th st of the Mane Piece, and sc across both sides) repeat for each Mane Piece (28 sts) (see images 3-4 above).

Fasten off and leave a 12-inch (30.5-cm) tail. Do not stuff.

## Horns (make 2)

In C2, ch 2, then sc 4 into the second ch away from hook (4 sts).

**Rnd 1:** Inc in each st (8 sts).

**Rnd 2-3:** Sc in each st (8 sts).

**Rnd 4:** Dec 4 times (4 sts). Break C2.

**Rnds 5–9:** With MC, sc in each st (4 sts).

Fasten off and leave a 6-inch (15-cm) tail for sewing.

## Assembly

Sew the Mane to the Neck of the Giraffe, starting from Rnd 22 of the Neck to Rnd 30 of the Neck. Sew the Horns 5 sts apart on Rnd 30 of the Head. Sew each Ear 2 sts apart from each Horn. Finally, sew the Tail to the back of the Body, on Rnd 16. Weave in all ends.

If you prefer to embroider the eyes instead of using safety eyes, set them 15 sts apart on Rnd 9 of the Head (for more information on sewing eyes onto plushies, see page 13).

# Miso the Monkey

This is a beginner pattern of a classic jungle animal—and you only need to sew the ears to the monkey! Miso is one of the easiest patterns in this book, so you'll be able to crochet without stress and create this huggable friend.

## Skill Level
Beginner

## Size
Approx 6 inches (15 cm) long, 7 inches (18 cm) wide and 10 inches (25.5 cm) tall

## Yarn
Super chunky chenille yarn, Premier Yarns Parfait Chunky, 100% polyester, 131 yds (120 m) and 3.5 oz (100 g) per skein

- Toffee (MC), 2 skeins, 262 yds (240 m) total
- Cream (C1), ½ skein, approx 66 yds (60 m) total

## Hooks
US size H-8 (5mm)

## Notions
Polyester fiberfill
Removable marker used to mark the first stitch of the round
Tapestry needle
Pair of 6mm safety eyes (optional)

## Gauge
20 sc x 5 rounds = 4 inches (10 cm)

## Abbreviations
**C1** = color 1
**Ch(s)** = chain(s)
**Dec** = decrease (crochet 2 sc together)
**Flo** = front loop only
**Inc** = increase (work 2 sc into one stitch)
**MC** = main color
**Sc** = single crochet
**St(s)** = stitch(es)

## Pattern Stitches
**Puff Stitch** = Yarn over, insert your hook through the st, yarn over and then draw up a loop. Repeat until you have 6 loops on the hook. Yarn over and draw through all 6 loops.

## Arms (make 2)

With C1, ch 2 and inc 3 times in the 2nd ch away from hook (6 sts).

**Rnd 1:** Inc 6 times (12 sts).

**Rnd 2:** Sc 8, Puff st, sc 3 (12 sts).

**Rnd 3:** Sc in each st (12 sts). Break C1.

**Rnds 4–9:** With MC, sc in each st (12 sts).

**Rnd 10:** (Dec, sc) 4 times (8 sts).

**Rnds 11–17:** Sc in each st (8 sts). Stuff the Arms only on Rnds 1–10.

**Rnd 18:** Ch 1. Fold the Arm in half side to side, and sc across both sides (4 sts).

Fasten off and leave a 3-inch (7.5-cm) tail. Do not stuff.

## Legs (make 2)

With C1, ch 2 and inc 3 times in the 2nd ch away from hook (6 sts).

**Rnd 1:** Inc 6 times (12 sts).

**Rnds 2–3:** Sc in each st (12 sts). Break C1.

**Rnds 4–11:** With MC, sc in each st (12 sts).

Fasten off and leave a 3-inch (7.5-cm) tail. Do not stuff.

## Ears (make 2)

With MC, ch 2 and inc 3 times in the 2nd ch away from hook (6 sts).

**Rnd 1:** Inc 6 times (12 sts).

**Rnd 2:** With MC, sc. With C1, sc, inc, sc. With MC, sc, (inc, sc 2) 2 times, inc (16 sts).

**Rnd 3:** With MC, sc. With C1, sc 5. With MC, sc 10 (16 sts).

**Rnd 4:** With MC, sc. With C1, sc 6. With MC, sc 9 (16 sts).

**Rnd 5:** Ch 1. Fold the Ear in half side to side, and sc across both sides (8 sts) (for more information on sc across both sides, see Gale the Giraffe, page 59).

Fasten off and leave a 6-inch (15-cm) tail. Do not stuff.

## Tail

With MC, ch 2 and inc 3 times in the 2nd ch away from hook (6 sts).

**Rnds 1–15:** Sc in each st (6 sts).

Fasten off and leave a 3-inch (7.5-cm) tail. Do not stuff.

## Body and Head

With MC, ch 2 and inc 4 times in the 2nd ch away from hook (8 sts).

**Rnd 1:** Inc 8 times (16 sts).

**Rnd 2:** (Sc, inc) 8 times (24 sts).

**Rnd 3:** Sc 4, attach Leg with 4 sts, sc 8, attach Leg with 4 sts, sc 4 (24 sts).

**Rnd 5:** Sc in the first 4 sts of the Body. Sc in the remaining 8 sts of the Leg. Sc in the next 8 sts of the Body. Sc in the remaining 8 sts of the Leg. Sc in the last 4 sts of the Body (32 sts).

**Rnd 6:** (Inc, sc 3) 8 times (40 sts).

**Rnd 7:** Sc 20, attach Tail with 2 sts, sc 18 (40 sts).

**Rnd 8:** Sc in the first 20 sts of the Body. Sc in the remaining 4 sts of the Tail. Sc in the remaining 18 sts of the Body (42 sts).

**Rnds 9–15:** Sc in each st (42 sts).

**Rnd 16:** (Dec, sc 5) 6 times (36 sts).

**Rnds 17–18:** Sc in each st (36 sts).

**Rnd 19:** (Dec, sc 4) 6 times (30 sts).

**Rnds 20–21:** Sc in each st (30 sts).

**Rnd 22:** (Dec, sc 3) 6 times (24 sts). Stuff the Legs and Body.

**Rnd 23:** Sc in each st (24 sts).

**Rnd 24:** (Dec, sc 2) 6 times (18 sts).

**Rnd 25:** Sc 5, attach Arm with 4 sts, sc 5, attach Arm with 4 sts (18 sts).

**Rnd 26:** Sc in each st (18 sts).

**Rnd 27:** With MC, inc in the flo. With C1, inc 5 times. With MC, sc 12 (24 sts).

**Rnd 28:** With MC, inc, sc. With C1, sc, (inc, sc) 5 times. With MC, sc 11 (30 sts).

**Rnd 29:** With MC, inc, sc 2. With C1, sc 2, (inc, sc 4) 3 times. With MC, (inc, sc 4) 2 times (36 sts).

**Rnds 30–31:** With MC, sc 4. With C1, sc 19. With MC, sc 13 (36 sts).

**Rnd 32:** With MC, sc 5. With C1, sc 18. With MC, sc 13 (36 sts).

**Rnd 33:** With MC, sc 6. With C1, (dec, sc) 5 times, dec. With MC, sc 13 (30 sts).

**Rnd 34:** With MC, sc 6. With C1, sc 11. With MC, sc 13 (30 sts).

**Rnd 35:** With MC, sc 6. With C1, dec 6 times. With MC, sc 12 (24 sts).

**Rnd 36:** With MC, sc 6. With C1, sc 7. With MC, sc 11 (24 sts).

**Rnd 37:** With MC, sc 6. With C1, sc 8. With MC, sc 10 (24 sts). If using safety eyes, attach them on this round, 4 sts apart.

**Rnd 38:** With MC, sc 7. With C1, sc 3. With MC, sc. With C1, sc 3. With MC, sc 10 (24 sts). Break C1.

**Rnd 39:** With MC, sc in each st (24 sts). Stuff the Head.

**Rnd 40:** (Dec, sc 2) 6 times (24 sts).

**Rnd 41:** Sc in each st (18 sts).

**Rnd 42:** (Dec, sc) 6 times (12 sts).

**Rnd 43:** Dec 6 times (6 sts).

Fasten off and sew the hole closed.

## Assembly

Sew the Ears to the side of the Head, aligning with Rnds 30–37. Weave in all ends.

If you prefer to embroider the eyes instead of using safety eyes, set them 4 sts apart on Rnd 37 (for more information on embroidering eyes, see page 13).

# Ellie the Elephant

This elephant will remember all the memories that you make with it! If you'd like a longer trunk, feel free to add extra rows at the base.

## Skill Level
Beginner

## Size
Approx 14 inches (35.5 cm) long, 7 inches (18 cm) wide and 10 inches (25 cm) tall

## Yarn
Super chunky chenille yarn, Premier Yarns Parfait Chunky, 100% polyester, 131 yds (120 m) and 3.5 oz (100 g) per skein

- Light Blue (MC), 2 skeins, 262 yds (240 m) total
- Cornflower (C1), ½ skein, approx 66 yds (60 m) total

## Hooks
US size H-8 (5mm)

## Notions
Polyester fiberfill
Removable marker used to mark the first stitch of the round
Tapestry needle
Pair of 10mm safety eyes (optional)

## Gauge
10 sc x 5 rounds = 4 inches (10 cm)

### Abbreviations
**Blo** = back loop only
**C1** = color 1
**Ch(s)** = chain(s)
**Dec** = decrease (crochet 2 sc together)
**Flo** = front loop only
**Inc** = increase (work 2 sc into one stitch)
**MC** = main color
**Sc** = single crochet
**St(s)** = stitch(es)

### Pattern Stitches
**Puff Stitch** = Yarn over, insert your hook through the st, yarn over and then draw up a loop. Repeat until you have 6 loops on the hook. Yarn over and draw through all 6 loops.

## Legs (make 4)

With C1, ch 2 and inc 3 times in the 2nd ch away from hook (6 sts).

**Rnd 1:** Inc in each st (12 sts).

**Rnd 2:** Sc in the blo of each st (12 sts). Break C1.

**Rnd 3:** With MC, sc in the blo of each st (12 sts).

**Rnds 4–6:** Sc in each st (12 sts).

Fasten off and leave a 6-inch (15-cm) tail.

## Tail

With MC, ch 6. Puff st in the 2nd ch from hook and sc in the remaining 4 chs. Fasten off and leave a 6-inch (15-cm) tail.

## Body

With MC, ch 10. Inc in the 2nd ch from hook, sc in the next 7 chs, and inc 2 times in the last ch. Turn your work clockwise 180 degrees, so that you can work along the opposite side of the ch. Then, sc in the next 7 chs, and inc in the last ch (22 sts).

**Rnd 1:** Inc in the first 2 sts, sc 7, inc in the next 4 sts, sc 7, inc in the last 2 sts (30 sts).

**Rnd 2:** (Sc 2, attach Leg with 3 sts, sc 5, attach the next Leg with 3 sts, sc 2) 2 times (30 sts) (for more information on attaching legs, see page 10).

**Rnd 3:** (Sc in the first 2 sts of the Body, sc in the remaining 9 sts of the Leg, sc in the next 5 sts of the Body, sc in the remaining 9 sts of the next Leg, sc in the next 2 sts of the Body) 2 times (54 sts).

**Rnd 4:** (Inc, sc 8) 6 times (60 sts).

**Rnds 5–9:** Sc in each st (60 sts).

**Rnd 10:** (Dec, sc 8) 6 times (54 sts).

**Rnds 11–13:** Sc in each st (54 sts). Lightly stuff the Body as you work.

**Rnd 14:** (Dec, sc 7) 6 times (48 sts).

**Rnds 15–16:** Sc in each st (48 sts).

**Rnd 17:** (Dec, sc 6) 6 times (42 sts).

**Rnd 18:** Sc in each st (42 sts).

**Rnd 19:** (Dec, sc 5) 6 times (36 sts). Stuff the Body.

**Rnd 20:** (Dec, sc 4) 6 times (30 sts).

**Rnd 21:** (Dec, sc 3) 6 times (24 sts).

**Rnd 22:** (Dec, sc 2) 6 times (18 sts).

**Rnd 23:** (Dec, sc) 6 times (12 sts).

**Rnd 24:** Dec 6 times (6 sts).

Fasten off and sew the hole closed.

## Ears (make 2)

With MC, ch 2 and inc 3 times in the 2nd ch away from hook (6 sts).

**Rnd 1:** Inc in each st (12 sts).

**Rnd 2:** (Inc, sc) 6 times (18 sts).

**Rnd 3:** (Inc, sc 2) 6 times (24 sts).

Fasten off and leave a 6-inch (15-cm) tail for sewing.

## Head

With MC, ch 2 and inc 3 times in the 2nd ch away from hook (6 sts).

**Rnds 1–2:** Sc in each st (6 sts). Feel free to add 1 or 2 more Rnds like these if you'd like a longer trunk.

**Rnd 3:** (Inc, sc 2) 2 times (8 sts).

**Rnds 4–5:** Sc in each st (8 sts).

**Rnd 5:** (Inc, sc) 4 times (12 sts).

**Rnd 6:** Sc in each st (12 sts).

**Rnd 7:** Dec 2 times, inc 4 times, dec 2 times (12 sts).

**Rnd 8:** Inc 12 times (24 sts).

**Rnd 9:** Sc 8, (inc, sc) 6 times, sc 4 (30 sts).

**Rnd 10:** Sc 8, (inc, sc 2) 6 times, sc 4 (36 sts).

**Rnds 11–15:** Sc in each st (36 sts).

**Rnd 16:** (Dec, sc 4) 6 times (30 sts).

**Rnd 17:** Sc in each st (30 sts).

Fasten off and leave a 12-inch (30.5-cm) tail for sewing.

## Assembly

Stuff the Head and sew the Head to the front of the Body on Rnds 5–16. Sew the Ears 12 sts apart on Rnd 8 of the Head. Sew the Tail to the back of the Body on Rnd 11. Finally, sew 2 consecutive sts of each Ear on Rnd 17 of the Head, making sure that the Ears are on opposite sides of each other 20 sts apart. Weave in all ends.

**Optional:** If you prefer to embroider the eyes instead of using safety eyes, set them 11 sts apart on Rnd 13 of the Head (for more information on embroidering eyes, see page 13).

# Ria the Rhinoceros

Although rhinos are known to live a solitary life, this rhino will love spending time snuggling with you! This pattern requires no color changing at all. Although it's a simple pattern, it creates the cuddliest rhino as a result!

## Skill Level
Beginner

## Size
Approx 14 inches (36 cm) long, 7 inches (18 cm) wide and 10 inches (25.5 cm) tall

## Yarn
Super chunky chenille yarn, Premier Yarns Parfait Chunky, 100% polyester, 131 yds (120 m) and 3.5 oz (100 g) per skein

- Light Gray (MC), 2 skeins, 262 yds (240 m) total
- Gray (C1), ½ skein, approx 66 yds (60 m) total
- Cream (C2), ½ skein, approx 66 yds (60 m) total

## Hooks
US size H-8 (5mm)

## Notions
Polyester fiberfill
Removable marker used to mark the first stitch of the round
Tapestry needle
Pair of 6mm safety eyes (optional)

## Gauge
10 sc x 5 rounds = 4 inches (10 cm)

## Abbreviations

**Blo** = back loop only

**C1** = color 1

**C2** = color 2

**Ch(s)** = chain(s)

**Dec** = decrease (crochet 2 sc together)

**Flo** = front loop only

**Inc** = increase (work 2 sc into one stitch)

**MC** = main color

**Sc** = single crochet

**St(s)** = stitch(es)

## Legs (make 4)

With C1, ch 2 and inc 3 times in the 2nd ch away from hook (6 sts).

**Rnd 1:** Inc in each st (12 sts).

**Rnd 2:** Sc in the blo of each st (12 sts). Break C1.

**Rnd 3:** With MC, sc in the blo of each st (12 sts).

**Rnd 4:** Sc in each st (12 sts).

Fasten off and leave a 6-inch (15-cm) tail.

## Tail

With MC, ch 2 and inc 3 times in the 2nd ch away from hook (6 sts).

**Rnd 1:** Sc in each st (6 sts).

**Rnd 2:** (Inc, sc 2) 2 times (8 sts).

**Rnds 3–7:** Sc in each st (8 sts).

**Rnd 8:** Fold the Tail in half, place your hook into the 1st and 8th st of the Tail, and sc across both sides. Fasten off and leave a 6-inch (15-cm) tail.

## Body

With MC, ch 10. Inc in the 2nd ch from hook, sc in the next 7 chs, and inc 2 times in the last ch. Turn your work clockwise 180 degrees, so that you can work along the opposite side of the ch. Then, sc in the next 7 chs, and inc in the last ch (22 sts).

**Rnd 1:** Inc in the first 2 sts, sc 7, inc in the next 4 sts, sc 7, inc in the last 2 sts (30 sts).

**Rnd 2:** (Sc 2, attach Leg with 3 sts, sc 5, attach the next Leg with 3 sts, sc 2) 2 times (30 sts) (for more information on attaching legs, see page 10).

**Rnd 3:** (Sc in the first 2 sts of the Body, sc in the remaining 9 sts of the Leg, sc in the next 5 sts of the Body, sc in the remaining 9 sts of the next Leg, sc in the next 2 sts of the Body) 2 times (54 sts).

**Rnd 4:** (Inc, sc 8) 6 times (60 sts).

**Rnds 5–10:** Sc in each st (60 sts).

**Rnd 11:** (Dec, sc 8) 6 times (54 sts).

**Rnds 12–13:** Sc in each st (54 sts). Lightly stuff the Body as you work.

**Rnd 14:** (Dec, sc 7) 6 times (48 sts).

**Rnds 15–16:** Sc in each st (48 sts). Place a removable marker on Rnd 16.

**Rnd 17:** (Dec, sc 6) 6 times (42 sts).

**Rnd 18:** Sc in each st (42 sts).

**Rnd 19:** (Dec, sc 5) 6 times (36 sts). Stuff the Body.

**Rnd 20:** (Dec, sc 4) 6 times (30 sts).

**Rnd 21:** (Dec, sc 3) 6 times (24 sts).

**Rnd 22:** (Dec, sc 2) 6 times (18 sts).

**Rnd 23:** (Dec, sc) 6 times (12 sts).

**Rnd 24:** Dec 6 times (6 sts).

Fasten off and sew the hole closed.

## Ears (make 2)

With C1, ch 2 and inc 3 times in the 2nd ch away from hook (6 sts).

**Rnd 1:** Inc in each st (12 sts).

Fasten off and leave a 3-inch (7.5-cm) tail.

## Head

With MC, ch 2 and inc 4 times in the 2nd ch away from hook (8 sts).

**Rnd 1:** Inc 8 times (16 sts).

**Rnd 2:** (Inc, sc) 8 times (24 sts).

**Rnds 3–7:** Sc in each st (24 sts).

**Rnd 8:** In the flo, (inc, sc 3) 6 times (30 sts).

**Rnds 9–12:** Sc in each st (30 sts). On Rnd 9, if using safety eyes, attach them on this round, 13 sts apart.

**Rnd 13:** (Dec, sc 3) 6 times (24 sts).

**Rnd 14:** Sc 10, attach Ear with 1 st, sc 6, attach 2nd Ear with 1 st, sc 6 (24 sts).

**Rnd 15:** Sc in each st (24 sts). Stuff the Head.

**Rnd 16:** (Dec, sc 2) 6 times (18 sts).

**Rnd 17:** (Dec, sc) 6 times (12 sts).

**Rnd 18:** Dec 6 times (6 sts).

Fasten off and leave an 8-inch (20.5-cm) tail.

## Horn A

With C2, ch 2 and inc 3 times in the 2nd ch away from hook (6 sts).

**Rnd 1:** (Inc, sc) 3 times (9 sts).

**Rnds 2–4:** Sc in each st (9 sts).

Fasten off and leave a 6-inch (15-cm) tail. Stuff the Horn.

## Horn B

With C2, ch 2 and inc 3 times in the 2nd ch away from hook (6 sts).

**Rnd 1:** Sc in each st (6 sts).

**Rnd 2:** (Inc, sc 2) 2 times (8 sts).

Fasten off and leave a 6-inch (15-cm) tail. Stuff the Horn.

## Assembly

Sew the Head to the front of the Body on Rnds 14–17. Then, sew Horn A to Rnds 3–5 of the Head. Sew Horn B to Rnds 9–11 of the Head. Sew the Tail to the back of the Body on Rnd 12. Weave in all ends.

If you prefer to embroider the eyes instead of using safety eyes, set them 13 sts apart on Rnd 9 of the Head (for more information on embroidering eyes, see page 13).

# Bibi the Bird

Crochet yourself a super colorful friend! Birds are very intelligent, but it won't take you too much brainpower to work up Bibi the Bird for yourself. Feel free to make multiple birds with different color schemes, just like the birds in the wild!

## Skill Level
Beginner

## Size
Approx 14 inches (35.5 cm) long, 7 inches (18 cm) wide and 10 inches (25.5 cm) tall

## Yarn
Super chunky chenille yarn, Premier Yarns Parfait Chunky, 100% polyester, 131 yds (120 m) and 3.5 oz (100 g) per skein

- Coral (MC), 2 skeins, 262 yds (240 m) total
- Lime Green (C1), ½ skein, approx 66 yds (60 m) total
- Sunshine (C2), ⅓ skein, 44 yds (40 m) total
- Mint (C3), ⅓ skein, 44 yds (40 m) total
- Scarlet (C4), ⅓ skein, 44 yds (40 m) total

## Hooks
US size H-8 (5mm)

## Notions
Polyester fiberfill
Removable marker used to mark the first stitch of the round
Tapestry needle
Pair of 10mm safety eyes (optional)

## Gauge
10 sc x 5 rounds = 4 inches (10 cm)

### Abbreviations
C1 = color 1
C2 = color 2
C3 = color 3
C4 = color 4
Ch(s) = chain(s)
Dec = decrease (crochet 2 sc together)
Flo = front loop only
Inc = increase (work 2 sc into one stitch)
MC = main color
Sc = single crochet
St(s) = stitch(es)

## Legs (make 2)

With C2, ch 2, and sc 8 into the second ch away from hook (8 sts).

**Rnds 1–3:** Sc in each st (8 sts).

**Rnd 4:** Ch 1. Fold the Leg in half side to side, and sc across through both sides (for more information on sc across both sides, see Gale the Giraffe, page 59).

Fasten off and leave a 3-inch (7.5-cm) tail. Do not stuff.

## Tail

With C1, ch 2 and inc 3 times in the 2nd ch away from hook (6 sts).

**Rnd 1:** Sc in each st (6 sts).

**Rnd 2:** (Inc, sc 2) 2 times (8 sts).

**Rnd 3:** (Inc, sc 3) 2 times (10 sts).

**Rnd 4:** (Inc, sc 4) 2 times (12 sts). Stuff the Tail.

**Rnd 5:** Sc in each st (12 sts).

Fasten off and leave a 6-inch (15-cm) tail for sewing.

## Beak

With C4, ch 2 and inc 3 times in the 2nd ch away from hook (6 sts).

**Rnd 1:** Sc in each st (6 sts).

**Rnd 2:** (Inc, sc 2) 2 times (8 sts).

**Rnd 3:** (Inc, sc 3) 2 times (10 sts). Stuff the Beak.

Fasten off and leave a 6-inch (15-cm) tail for sewing.

## Wings (make 2)

With C1, ch 2 and inc 3 times in the 2nd ch away from hook (6 sts).

**Rnd 1:** Sc in each st (6 sts).

**Rnd 2:** Sc 2, inc 3 times in the flo, sc (9 sts).

**Rnd 3:** Sc 2, in the flo (inc, sc) 3 times, sc (12 sts).

**Rnd 4:** (Inc, sc 2) 4 times (16 sts).

**Rnds 5–6:** Sc in each st (16 sts).

**Rnd 7:** Sc 9, inc 4 times in the flo, sc 3 (20 sts).

**Rnd 8:** Sc 9, in the flo (inc, sc) 4 times, sc 3 (24 sts).

**Rnd 9:** Sc in each st (24 sts).

**Rnd 10:** (Dec, sc 2) 6 times (18 sts).

**Rnd 11:** Sc in each st (18 sts).

**Rnd 12:** (Dec, sc) 6 times (12 sts).

**Rnd 13:** Dec 6 times (6 sts).

Fasten off and leave a 6-inch (15-cm) tail for sewing. Fold in half, so the curves of the Wing are visible. Do not stuff.

## Body

With MC, ch 2 and inc 3 times in the 2nd ch away from hook (6 sts).

**Rnd 1:** Inc 6 times (12 sts).

**Rnd 2:** (Inc, sc) 6 times (18 sts).

**Rnd 3:** (Inc, sc 2) 6 times (24 sts).

**Rnd 4:** (Inc, sc 3) 6 times (30 sts).

**Rnd 5:** (Inc, sc 4) 6 times (36 sts).

**Rnds 6–10:** Sc in each st (36 sts).

**Rnd 11:** (Dec, sc 4) 6 times (30 sts).

**Rnd 12:** Sc in each st (30 sts).

**Rnd 13:** (Dec, sc 3) 6 times (24 sts).

**Rnd 14:** (Dec, sc) 8 times (16 sts). Break MC.

**Rnd 15:** With C1, (sc, inc) 3 times. With C3, (sc, inc) 2 times. With C1, (sc, inc) 3 times (24 sts).

**Rnd 16:** With C1, (inc, sc 3) 2 times, inc. With C3, sc 3, inc, sc 3. With C1, (inc, sc 3) 2 times (30 sts).

**Rnd 17:** With C1, sc 3, inc, sc 4, inc, sc 3. With C3, sc, inc, sc 4, inc, sc. With C1, sc 3, inc, sc 4, inc, sc (36 sts).

**Rnd 18:** With C1, sc 14. With C3, sc 10. With C1, sc 12 (36 sts). At this time, if using safety eyes, attach them on Rnd 8, 6 sts apart.

**Rnd 19:** With C1, sc 15. With C3, sc 10. With C1, sc 11 (36 sts).

**Rnd 20:** With C1, sc 16. With C3, sc 10. With C1, sc 10 (36 sts).

**Rnd 21:** With C1, sc 16. With C3, sc 10. With C1, sc 10 (36 sts).

**Rnd 22:** With C1, (inc, sc 5) 2 times, inc, sc 4. With C3, sc, inc, sc 5, inc, sc. With C1, sc 4, inc, sc 5 (42 sts).

**Rnd 23:** With C1, sc 21. With C3, sc 10. With C1, sc 11 (42 sts).

**Rnd 24:** With C1, sc 23. With C3, sc 7. With C1, sc 12 (42 sts).

**Rnd 25:** With C1, sc 24. With C3, sc 5. With C1, sc 13 (42 sts). Break C3.

**Rnd 26:** With C1, (dec, sc 5) 6 times (36 sts).

**Rnd 27:** (Dec, sc 4) 6 times (30 sts). Stuff the Head and Body.

**Rnd 28:** Sc 2, (dec, sc 3) 5 times, dec, sc (24 sts).

**Rnd 28:** Sc 10, attach the Leg with 4 sts, sc 4, attach Leg with 4 sts, sc 2 (24 sts) (for more information on attaching legs, see page 10).

**Rnd 29:** (Dec, sc 2) 6 times (18 sts).

**Rnd 30:** (Dec, sc) 6 times (12 sts).

**Rnd 31:** Dec 6 times (6 sts).

Fasten off and sew the hole closed.

## Assembly

Sew each Wing to opposite sides of the Body, right next to the oval made with C3. Make sure that the curves of the Wings face the bottom. Sew the Tail to the back of the Body, approximately at Rnd 23. Sew the Beak on Rnds 8–11 of the Head, in the middle. Weave in all ends.

If you prefer to embroider the eyes instead of using safety eyes, set them 2 sts apart from each side of the Beak on Rnd 8 of the Head (for more information on sewing eyes onto plushies, see page 13).

# Farm Pals

Welcome to the lively bustle of a farm! The air smells fresh and is filled with the sounds of clucking chickens and mooing cows. Pastures stretch as far as the eye can see. The farm is a bundle of life! From pigs to horses, each animal has its place and purpose and is special in its own way.

Imagine crocheting your own farm, crafting each piece with yarn and hook. Your creations could be a cute toy set for a toddler in your life to teach them about the sounds of the farm. Or maybe there is a child in your life who would be thrilled to be given a handmade horse. Whatever the case may be, you'll enjoy making each animal. Keep in mind, some of these animals have a lot more pieces that need to be sewn to make the final plushie, but luckily any mistakes made during sewing will be easily forgiven due to the nature of each body piece.

# Cleo the Cow

Moo! Cleo is a classic farm animal. Although you probably don't have a farm, you'll soon have your own cow! You'll have to test your color-changing skills with this one, but once you finish this cow, you'll realize that it wasn't as hard as you thought.

## Skill Level
Intermediate

## Size
Approx 8 inches (20.5 cm) long, 9 inches (23 cm) wide and 8 inches (20.5 cm) tall

## Yarn
Super chunky chenille yarn, Premier Yarns Parfait Chunky, 100% polyester, 131 yds (120 m) and 3.5 oz (100 g) per skein

- White (MC), 2 skeins, 262 yds (240 m) total
- Black (C1), ½ skein, approx 66 yds (60 m) total
- Ballet Pink (C2), ½ skein, approx 66 yds (60 m) total

## Hooks
US size H-8 (5mm)

## Notions
Polyester fiberfill
Removable marker used to mark the first stitch of the round
Tapestry needle
Pair of 6mm safety eyes (optional)

## Gauge
10 sc x 5 rounds = 4 inches (10 cm)

### Abbreviations
C1 = color 1
C2 = color 2
Ch(s) = chain(s)
Dec = decrease (crochet 2 sc together)
Inc = increase (work 2 sc into one stitch)
MC = main color
Sc = single crochet
Sl st = slip stitch
St(s) = stitch(es)

### Pattern Stitches
**Puff Stitch** = Yarn over, insert your hook through the st, yarn over and then draw up a loop. Repeat until you have 6 loops on the hook. Yarn over and draw through all 6 loops.

## Legs (make 4)

With C1, ch 2 and inc 3 times in the 2nd ch away from hook (6 sts).

**Rnd 1:** Inc in each st (12 sts).

**Rnd 2:** In the blo, sc in each st (12 sts). Break C1.

**Rnds 3–5:** With MC, sc in each st (12 sts).

Fasten off and leave a 6-inch (15-cm) tail.

## Body

With MC, ch 5. Inc in the 2nd ch from hook, sc in the next 2 chs, and inc 2 times in the last ch. Turn your work clockwise 180 degrees, so that you can work along the opposite side of the ch. Then, sc in the next 2 chs, and inc in the last ch (12 sts).

**Rnd 1:** Inc in the first st, sc 4, inc into the next 2 st, sc 4, inc into the last st (16 sts).

**Rnd 2:** Sc in first st, attach Leg 1 with 2 sts, (sc 2, attach the next Leg with 2 sts) 2 times, sc 2, attach Leg 4 with 2 sts, sc in last st (16 sts) (for more information on attaching legs, see page 10).

**Rnd 3:** Sc in first st, (sc in the remaining 10 sts of the next Leg, sc 2) 3 times, sc in remaining 10 sts of last Leg, sc 1 (48 sts).

**Rnd 4:** Sc in each st (48 sts).

**Rnd 5:** With MC, sc 9. With C1, sc 6. With MC, sc 13. With C1, sc 5. With MC, sc 12. With C1, sc 3 (48 sts).

**Rnd 6:** With C1, sc 2. With MC, sc 6. With C1, sc 8. With MC, sc 12. With C1, sc 6. With MC, sc 11. With C1, sc 3 (48 sts).

**Rnd 7:** With C1, sc 3. With MC, sc 5. With C1, sc 9. With MC, sc 11. With C1, sc 7. With MC, sc 10. With C1, sc 3 (48 sts).

**Rnd 8:** With C1, sc 3. With MC, sc 6. With C1, sc 8. With MC, sc 12. With C1, sc 6. With MC, sc 11. With C1, sc 2 (48 sts).

**Rnd 9:** With C1, sc 3. With MC, sc 7. With C1, sc 6. With MC, sc 4. With C1, sc 5. With MC, sc 5. With C1, sc 5. With MC, sc 4. With C1, sc 4. With MC, sc 4. With C1, sc (48 sts).

**Rnd 10:** With C1, sc 2. With MC, sc 3. With C1, sc 4. With MC, sc 2. With C1, sc 4. With MC, sc 5. With C1, sc 6. With C1, sc 5. With C1, sc 3. With MC, sc 5. With C1, sc 5. With MC, sc 4 (48 sts).

**Rnd 11:** With MC, sc 5. With C1, sc 5. With MC, sc 10. With C1, sc 6. With MC, sc 13. With C1, sc 6. With MC, sc 3 (48 sts).

**Rnd 12:** With MC, sc 5. With C1, sc 5. With MC, sc 11. With C1, sc 5. With MC, sc 14. With C1, sc 5. With MC, sc 3 (48 sts). Stuff the Legs.

**Rnd 13:** With MC, sc 6. With C1, sc 4. With MC, sc 12. With, C1 sc 3. With MC, sc 16. With C1, sc 3. With MC, sc 4 (48 sts).

**Rnd 14:** With MC, dec, sc 5. With C1, sc, dec. With MC, sc 6, (dec, sc 6) 4 times (42 sts). Break C1.

**Rnd 15:** With MC, sc in each st (42 sts).

**Rnd 16:** (Dec, sc 5) 6 times (36 sts).

**Rnd 17:** (Dec, sc 4) 6 times (30 sts). Stuff the Body.

**Rnd 18:** (Dec, sc 3) 6 times (24 sts).

**Rnd 19:** (Dec, sc 2) 6 times (18 sts).

**Rnd 20:** (Dec, sc) 6 times (12 sts).

**Rnd 21:** Dec 6 times (6 sts).

Fasten off and leave a 6-inch (15-cm) tail.

## Ears (make 2)

With MC, ch 2 and inc 3 times in the 2nd ch away from hook (6 sts).

**Rnd 1:** Inc in each st (12 sts).

Fasten off and leave a 6-inch (15-cm) tail.

## Tail

With MC, ch 6. Puff st in the 2nd ch from hook, sc 4 (5 sts).

Fasten off and leave a 6-inch (15-cm) tail.

## Head

With C2, ch 7. Inc in the 2nd ch from hook, sc in the next 4 chs, and inc 2 times in the last ch. Turn your work clockwise 180 degrees, so that you can work along the opposite side of the ch. Then, sc in the next 4 chs, and inc in the last ch (16 sts).

**Rnd 1:** (Inc, sc) 8 times (24 sts).

**Rnds 2–3:** Sc in each st (24 sts). Place a removable marker on this Rnd. Break C2.

**Rnds 4–5:** With MC, sc in each st (24 sts).

**Rnd 6:** With MC, sc 5. With C1, sc 4. With MC, sc 15 (24 sts).

**Rnds 7–8:** With MC, sc 4. With C1, sc 6. With MC, sc 14 (24 sts).

**Rnd 9:** With MC, dec, sc 2. With C1, dec, sc 2, dec. With MC, (sc 2, dec) 3 times, sc 2 (18 sts). Break C1.

**Rnd 10:** With MC, sc 4, Puff st, sc 3, Puff st, sc 9 (18 sts). Stuff the Head.

**Rnd 11:** Sc in each st (18 sts).

**Rnd 12:** (Dec, sc) 6 times (12 sts).

**Rnd 13:** Dec 6 times (6 sts).

Fasten off and leave a 6-inch (15-cm) tail. Sew the hole closed.

## Assembly

Sew the Head onto the front of the Body, aligning the Head toward the top of the Body so that Rnd 9 of the Head is aligned with Rnd 13 of the Body. Sew the Ears onto the sides of the Head, just below each Puff st on Rnd 8 of the Head. Then, embroider a nose onto the face as horizontal lines between Rnds 2 and 3 of the Head (removable marker shows these Rnds). Sew the Tail to the back of the Body. Weave in all ends.

**Optional:** If you prefer to embroider the eyes instead of using safety eyes, set them 3 sts apart on Rnd 5 of the Head (for more information on sewing eyes onto plushies, see page 13).

# Fido the Dog

Say hello to your new best friend! Your sweet crocheted dog will be loyal to you for decades to come. This pattern can be customized in so many ways because it's written as a blank slate. If you have a loved one that walks on all fours, try to make them next!

## Skill Level
Intermediate

## Size
Approx 14 inches (35.5 cm) long, 7 inches (18 cm) wide and 10 inches (25.5 cm) tall

## Yarn
Super chunky chenille yarn, Premier Yarns Parfait Chunky, 100% polyester, 131 yds (120 m) and 3.5 oz (100 g) per skein

- Toffee (MC), 2 skeins, 262 yds (240 m) total
- Teddy Bear (C1), ½ skein, approx 66 yds (60 m) total

## Hooks
US size H-8 (5mm)

## Notions
Polyester fiberfill
Removable marker used to mark the first stitch of the round
Tapestry needle
Pair of 10mm safety eyes (optional)

## Gauge
10 sc x 5 rounds = 4 inches (10 cm)

## Abbreviations

**Blo** = back loop only

**C1** = color 1

**Ch(s)** = chain(s)

**Dec** = decrease (crochet 2 sc together)

**Flo** = front loop only

**Inc** = increase (work 2 sc into one stitch)

**MC** = main color

**Sc** = single crochet

**Sl st** = slip stitch

**St(s)** = stitch(es)

## Legs (make 4)

With C1, ch 2 and inc 3 times in the 2nd ch away from hook (6 sts).

**Rnd 1:** Inc in each st (12 sts).

**Rnd 2:** Sc in the blo of each st (12 sts).

**Rnds 3–6:** With MC, sc in each st (12 sts).

Fasten off and leave a 6-inch (15-cm) tail for sewing.

## Tail

With MC, ch 2 and inc 3 times in the 2nd ch away from hook (6 sts).

**Rnds 1–10:** Sc in each st (6 sts).

Fasten off and leave a 6-inch (15-cm) tail for sewing. Do not stuff.

## Ears (make 2)

With MC, ch 2 and inc 3 times in the 2nd ch away from hook (6 sts).

**Rnd 1:** Sc in each st (6 sts).

**Rnd 2:** (Inc, sc) 3 times (9 sts).

**Rnd 3:** (Inc, sc 2) 3 times (12 sts).

**Rnd 4:** (Inc, sc 3) 3 times (15 sts).

**Rnd 5:** (Inc, sc 4) 3 times (18 sts).

**Rnd 6:** Sc in each st (18 sts).

**Rnd 7:** (Dec, sc 4) 3 times (15 sts).

**Rnd 8:** (Dec, sc 3) 3 times (12 sts).

**Rnd 9:** Sc in each st (12 sts).

**Rnd 10:** (Dec, sc) 4 times (8 sts).

**Rnd 11:** Ch 1. Fold the Ear in half side to side, and sc across through both sides (for more information on sc across both sides, see Gale the Giraffe, page 59).

Fasten off and leave a 6-inch (15-cm) tail for sewing. Do not stuff.

## Body

With MC, ch 13. Inc in the 2nd ch from hook, sc in the next 10 chs, and inc 2 times in the last ch. Turn your work clockwise 180 degrees, so that you can work along the opposite side of the ch. Then sc in the next 10 chs, and inc in the last ch (28 sts).

**Rnd 1:** Inc in the next 2 sts, sc 10, inc in the next 4 sts, sc 10, 2 inc (36 sts).

**Rnd 2:** (Sc 2, attach Leg with 3 sts, sc 8, attach the next Leg with 3 sts, sc 2) 2 times (36 sts) (for more information on attaching legs, see page 10).

**Rnd 3:** (Sc in the next 2 sts of the Body, sc in the remaining 9 sts of the next Leg, sc in the next 8 sts of the Body, sc in the remaining 9 sts of the next Leg, sc in the next 2 sts of the Body) 2 times (60 sts).

**Rnds 4–10:** Sc in each st (60 sts).

**Rnd 11:** Sc 20, (dec, sc 4) 4 times, sc 16 (56 sts).

**Rnds 12–13:** Sc in each st (56 sts).

**Rnd 14:** Sc 10, (dec, sc 3) 8 times, sc 6 (48 sts).

**Rnd 15:** Sc in each st (48 sts).

**Rnd 16:** Sc 14, (dec, sc 2) 6 times, sc 10 (42 sts). Stuff lightly as you work.

**Rnd 17:** Sc in each st (42 sts).

**Rnd 18:** Sc 14, (dec, sc) 6 times, sc 10 (36 sts).

**Rnd 19:** Sc 16, dec in the next 4 sts, sc 12 (32 sts).

**Rnd 20:** Sc 18. Place your hook into the flo of the 19th and 20th st (3 sts on hook). Sl st the sts together. Repeat this for the 18th and 21st st, the 17th and 22nd st, the 16th and 23rd st, the 15th and the 24th st, the 14th and the 25th st, the 13th and the 26th st, and the 12th and 27th st (for more information on closing off a body, see Flynn the Fox, page 29). Sc in the 28th st, and the remaining 15 sts that were left untouched (16 sts). Stuff the Body. Overstuff the Body on Rnds 18–20.

**Rnd 21:** Sc in each st (16 sts). This is the Neck portion.

Fasten off and leave a 6-inch (15-cm) tail for sewing. Finish stuffing the Body and Neck.

## Head

With MC, ch 2 and inc 3 times in the 2nd ch away from hook (6 sts).

**Rnd 1:** (Sc 3 in the next st, sc) 3 times (12 sts).

**Rnd 2:** (Sc, sc 3 in the next st, sc 2) 3 times (18 sts).

**Rnds 3–5:** Sc in each st (18 sts).

**Rnd 6:** Sc 8, inc in the flo in the next 2 sts, sc 3 in the next st, inc in the next 2 sts, sc 5 (24 sts). Stuff lightly as you work.

**Rnd 7:** (Sc 3, inc) 6 times (30 sts).

**Rnds 8–13:** Sc in each st (30 sts). Add safety eyes 12 sts apart on Rnd 8.

**Rnd 14:** (Dec, sc 3) 6 times (24 sts).

**Rnd 15:** Sc in each st (24 sts).

**Rnd 16:** (Dec, sc 2) 6 times (18 sts). Finish stuffing the Head.

**Rnd 17:** (Dec, sc) 6 times (12 sts).

**Rnd 18:** Dec 6 times (6 sts).

Fasten off and sew the hole closed.

## Assembly

Sew the Head to the top of the Body. When aligning it to the Neck, make sure to sew Rnds 6–10 of the Head to the Neck. Embroider a triangle-shaped nose onto the face, covering Rnds 1–3 of the Head (for more information on embroidering the nose, refer to this technique in Rae the Raccoon, page 23). Sew the Tail to the back of the Body, approximately at Rnd 11. Finally, sew each Ear to each side of the Head, making sure that the last Rnd of each Ear is about 1 inch (3 cm) above the Nose on Rnd 11 of the Head. Weave in all ends.

**Optional:** If you prefer to embroider the eyes instead of using safety eyes, set them 12 sts apart on Rnd 8 of the Head (for more information on sewing eyes onto plushies, see page 13).

# Callie the Cat

If you're a cat lover, this pattern is for you. Similar to Fido the Dog's pattern, this one is deliberately written as a blank slate so you can customize it to reflect a cat in your life! You'll get to practice your embroidery skills as you create the cat's nose.

## Skill Level
Intermediate

## Size
Approx 14 inches (35.5 cm) long, 7 inches (18 cm) wide and 10 inches (25.5 cm) tall

## Yarn
Super chunky chenille yarn, Premier Yarns Parfait Chunky, 100% polyester, 131 yds (120 m) and 3.5 oz (100 g) per skein

- Mustard (MC), 2 skeins, 262 yds (240 m) total
- Cream (C1), ½ skein, approx 66 yds (60 m) total
- Teddy Bear (C2), ⅓ skein, 44 yds (40 m) total

## Hooks
US size H-8 (5mm)

## Notions
Polyester fiberfill
Removable marker used to mark the first stitch of the round
Tapestry needle
Pair of 10mm safety eyes (optional)

## Gauge
10 sc x 5 rounds = 4 inches (10 cm)

### Abbreviations

**Blo** = back loop only

**C1** = color 1

**C2** = color 2

**Ch(s)** = chain(s)

**Dec** = decrease (crochet 2 sc together)

**Flo** = front loop only

**Inc** = increase (work 2 sc into one stitch)

**MC** = main color

**Sc** = single crochet

**Sl st** = slip stitch

**St(s)** = stitch(es)

## Legs (make 4)

With C2, ch 2 and inc 3 times in the 2nd ch away from hook (6 sts).

**Rnd 1:** Inc in each st (12 sts).

**Rnd 2:** Sc in the blo of each st (12 sts). Break C2.

**Rnds 3–5:** With MC, sc in each st (12 sts).

Fasten off and leave a 6-inch (15-cm) tail for sewing. Do not stuff.

## Tail

With MC, ch 2 and inc 3 times in the 2nd ch away from hook (6 sts).

**Rnds 1–3:** Sc in each st (6 sts).

**Rnd 4:** (Inc, sc 2) 2 times (8 sts).

**Rnds 5–8:** Sc in each st (8 sts).

**Rnd 9:** (Inc, sc 3) 2 times (10 sts).

**Rnd 10:** Sc in each st (10 sts).

Fasten off and leave a 6-inch (15-cm) tail for sewing. Do not stuff.

## Ears (make 2)

With MC, ch 2 and inc 2 times in the 2nd ch away from hook (4 sts).

**Rnd 1:** (Inc, sc) 2 times (6 sts).

**Rnd 2:** With MC, sc 2. With C1, sc. With MC, sc 3 (6 sts).

**Rnd 3:** With MC, sc 2. With C1, inc. With MC, sc 2, inc (8 sts).

**Rnd 4:** With MC, sc 2. With C1, sc, inc. With MC, sc 3, inc (10 sts). Break C1.

**Rnd 5:** With MC, ch 1. Fold the Ear in half side to side, and sc across through both sides (5 sts) (for more information on sc across both sides, see Gale the Giraffe, page 59).

Fasten off and leave a 6-inch (15-cm) tail for sewing. Do not stuff.

## Body

With C1, ch 13. Inc in the 2nd ch from hook, sc in the next 10 chs, and inc 2 times in the last ch. Turn your work clockwise 180 degrees, so that you can work along the opposite side of the ch. Then sc in the next 10 chs, and inc in the last ch (28 sts).

**Rnd 1:** Inc in the next 2 sts, sc 10, inc in the next 4 sts, sc 10, increase in the last 2 sts (36 sts).

**Rnd 2:** (Sc 2, attach Leg with 3 sts, sc 8, attach the next Leg with 3 sts, sc 2) 2 times (36 sts) (for more information on attaching legs, see page 10).

**Rnd 3:** (With C1, sc in the next 2 sts of the Body. With MC, sc in the remaining 9 sts of the next Leg. With MC, sc in the next 8 sts of the Body. With C1, sc in the remaining 9 sts of the next Leg. With MC, sc in the next 2 sts of the Body) 2 times (60 sts).

**Rnd 4:** With C1, sc 3. With MC, sc 54. With C1, sc 3 (60 sts).

**Rnds 5–6:** With C1, sc 4. With MC, sc 53. With C1, sc 3 (60 sts).

**Rnd 7:** With C1, sc 4. With MC, sc 54. With C1, sc 2 (60 sts).

**Rnd 8:** With C1, sc 4. With MC, sc 55. With C1, sc (60 sts).

**Rnd 9:** With C1, sc 4. With MC, sc 56 (60 sts). Break C1.

**Rnd 10:** With MC, sc in each st (60 sts).

**Rnd 11:** Sc 20, (dec, sc 4) 4 times, sc 16 (56 sts).

**Rnds 12–13:** Sc in each st (56 sts).

**Rnd 14:** Sc 10, (dec, sc 3) 8 times, sc 6 (48 sts).

**Rnd 15:** Sc in each st (48 sts).

**Rnd 16:** Sc 14, (dec, sc 2) 6 times, sc 10 (42 sts). Stuff lightly as you work.

**Rnd 17:** Sc in each st (42 sts).

**Rnd 18:** Sc 14, (dec, sc) 6 times, sc 10 (36 sts).

**Rnd 19:** Sc 16, dec 4 times, sc 12 (32 sts).

**Rnd 20:** Sc 18. Place your hook into the flo of the 19th and 20th st (3 sts on hook). Sl st the sts together. Repeat this for the 18th and 21st st, the 17th and 22nd st, the 16th and 23rd st, the 15th and 24th st, the 14th and 25th st, the 13th and 26th st, and the 12th and 27th st (for more information on closing off a body, see Flynn the Fox, page 29). Sc in the remaining 5 sts of this Rnd, and first 11 sts of the next Rnd. This is the new beginning of the Rnd (16 sts). Stuff the Body, overstuffing on Rnds 18–20.

**Rnd 21:** Sc in each st (16 sts). This is the Neck.

Fasten off and leave a 6-inch (15-cm) tail for sewing. Finish stuffing the Body and Neck.

## Head

With C1, ch 2 and inc 3 times in the 2nd ch away from hook (6 sts).

**Rnd 1:** (Inc, sc) 3 times (9 sts).

**Rnd 2:** (Inc, sc 2) 3 times (12 sts).

**Rnd 3:** With C1, sc 2. With MC, sc, inc in the next 6 sts, sc. With C1, sc 2 (18 sts).

**Rnd 4:** With C1, sc 2. With MC, sc 15. With C1, sc (18 sts).

**Rnd 5:** With C1, inc, sc. With MC, sc, (inc, sc 2) 5 times (24 sts). Break C1.

**Rnd 6:** With MC, (inc, sc 3) 6 times (30 sts).

**Rnds 7–9:** Sc in each st (30 sts).

**Rnd 10:** Sc 13. Attach Ear with 5 sts, sc 2, attach Ear 2 with 5 sts, sc 5 (30 sts).

**Rnd 11:** Sc in each st (30 sts).

**Rnd 12:** (Dec, sc 3) 6 times (24 sts).

**Rnd 13:** Sc in each st (24 sts). Stuff the Head.

**Rnd 14:** (Dec, sc 2) 6 times (18 sts).

**Rnd 15:** (Dec, sc) 6 times (12 sts).

**Rnd 16:** Dec 6 times (6 sts).

Fasten off and sew the hole closed.

## Assembly

Sew the Head to the top of the Body. When aligning it to the Neck, be sure to sew Rnds 6–11 of the Head to the Neck. With C2, embroider a triangle-shaped nose onto the face, covering Rnds 2–3 of the Head (see images 1–4 left). Finally, sew the Tail to the back of the Body, approximately at Rnd 13. Weave in all ends.

**Optional:** If you prefer to embroider the eyes instead of using safety eyes, set them 12 sts apart on Rnd 8 of the Head (for more information on sewing eyes onto plushies, see page 13).

# Penny the Pig

Another classic farm animal, this pig is a cute addition to any farm—or any bedroom! It's super big and cuddly, and it works up very fast because a majority of the pattern is worked with one color. You'll be pleased that a simple technique will make the curl of the pig's tail!

## Skill Level
Beginner

## Size
Approx 12 inches (30.5 cm) long, 9 inches (23 cm) wide and 8 inches (20.5 cm) tall

## Yarn
Super chunky chenille yarn, Premier Yarns Parfait Chunky, 100% polyester, 131 yds (120 m) and 3.5 oz (100 g) per skein

- Ballet Pink (MC), 2 skeins, 262 yds (240 m) total
- Hibiscus (C1), ½ skein, approx 66 yds (60 m) total

## Hooks
US size H-8 (5mm)

## Notions
Polyester fiberfill
Removable marker used to mark the first stitch of the round
Tapestry needle
Pair of 6mm safety eyes (optional)

## Gauge
10 sc x 5 rounds = 4 inches (10 cm)

### Abbreviations

**Blo** = back loop only

**C1** = color 1

**Ch(s)** = chain(s)

**Dec** = decrease (crochet 2 sc together)

**Flo** = front loop only

**Inc** = increase (work 2 sc into one stitch)

**MC** = main color

**Sc** = single crochet

**Sl st** = slip stitch

**St(s)** = stitch(es)

## Legs (make 4)

With C1, ch 2 and inc 3 times in the 2nd ch away from hook (6 sts).

**Rnd 1:** Inc in each st (12 sts).

**Rnd 2:** Sc in the blo of each st (12 sts).

**Rnd 3:** With MC, sc in each st (12 sts).

**Rnds 4–5:** Sc in each st (12 sts).

Fasten off and leave a 6-inch (15-cm) tail.

## Body

With MC, ch 10. Inc in the 2nd ch from hook, sc in the next 7 chs, and inc 2 times in the last ch. Turn your work clockwise 180 degrees, so that you can work along the opposite side of the ch. Then, sc in the next 7 chs, and inc in the last ch (22 sts).

**Rnd 1:** Inc in the first 2 sts, sc 7, inc in the next 4 sts, sc 7, inc in the last 2 sts (30 sts).

**Rnd 2:** (Sc 2, attach Leg with 3 sts, sc 5, attach the next Leg with 3 sts, sc 2) 2 times (30 sts) (for more information on attaching legs, see page 10).

**Rnd 3:** (Sc in the first 2 sts of the Body, sc in the remaining 9 sts of the Leg, sc in the next 5 sts of the Body, sc in the remaining 9 sts of the next Leg, sc in the next 2 sts of the Body) 2 times (54 sts).

**Rnd 4:** (Inc, sc 8) 6 times (60 sts).

**Rnds 5–7:** Sc in each st (60 sts).

**Rnd 8:** (Dec, sc 8) 6 times (54 sts).

**Rnds 9–10:** Sc in each st (54 sts). Lightly stuff the Body as you work.

**Rnd 11:** (Dec, sc 7) 6 times (48 sts).

**Rnd 12:** Sc in each st (48 sts). Place a removable marker on this Rnd.

**Rnd 13:** (Dec, sc 6) 6 times (42 sts).

**Rnds 14–15:** Sc in each st (42 sts).

**Rnd 16:** (Dec, sc 5) 6 times (36 sts). Stuff the Body.

**Rnd 17:** Sc in each st (36 st).

**Rnd 18:** (Dec, sc 4) 6 times (30 sts).

**Rnd 19:** (Dec, sc 3) 6 times (24 sts).

**Rnd 20:** (Dec, sc 2) 6 times (18 sts).

**Rnd 21:** (Dec, sc) 6 times (12 sts).

**Rnd 22:** Dec 6 times (6 sts).

Fasten off and sew the hole closed.

## Ears (make 2)

With MC, ch 2 and inc 3 times in the 2nd ch away from hook (6 sts).

**Rnd 1:** Sc in each st (6 sts).

**Rnd 2:** (Inc, sc) 3 times (9 sts).

**Rnd 3:** (Inc, sc 2) 3 times (12 sts).

**Rnd 4:** (Inc, sc 2) 4 times (16 sts).

**Rnd 5:** Ch 1. Fold the Ear in half side to side, and sc across through both sides (8 sts) (for more information on sc across both sides, see Gale the Giraffe, page 59).

Fasten off and leave a 6-inch (15-cm) tail. Do not stuff.

## Tail

With MC, ch 12. Inc in the 2nd ch from hook and the remaining 10 sts (22 sts).

Fasten off and leave a 6-inch (15-cm) tail.

## Head

With C1, ch 2 and inc 3 times in the 2nd ch away from hook (6 sts).

**Rnd 1:** (3 sc in one st, sc) 3 times (12 sts).

**Rnd 2:** (sc, 3 sc in one st, sc 2) 3 times (18 sts).

**Rnd 3:** In the flo, sc in each st (18 sts).

**Rnd 4:** Sc in each st (18 sts).

**Rnd 5:** (Place your hook into the flo of the next st and the blo of the next st from Rnd 3. Sc the sts together) 18 times (18 sts).

**Rnd 6:** Break C1. With MC in the flo, (sc 2, 3 sc in one st, sc 3) 3 times (24 sts).

**Rnd 7:** (Inc, sc 3) 6 times (30 sts).

**Rnd 8:** Sc 10, (inc, sc 2) 6 times, sc 2 (36 sts).

**Rnds 9–11:** Sc in each st (36 sts).

**Rnd 12:** Sc 13, attach Ear 1 with 8 sts, sc 4, attach Ear 2 with 8 sts, sc 3 (36 sts). Stuff the Head.

**Rnd 13:** Sc in each st (36 sts).

**Rnd 14:** Sc 12, (dec, sc 2) 6 times (30 sts).

**Rnd 15:** (Dec, sc 3) 6 times (24 sts).

Fasten off and leave a 12-inch (31-cm) tail.

## Assembly

Sew the last Rnd of the Head onto the front of the Body, aligning the Head toward the top of the Body so that Rnd 8 of the Head is aligned with Rnd 13 of the Body. Sew the Tail to the back of the Body on Rnd 10. Weave in all ends.

**Optional:** If you prefer to embroider the eyes instead of using safety eyes, set them 10 sts apart on Rnd 5 of the Head (for more information on sewing eyes onto plushies, see page 13). Weave in all ends.

# Henry the Horse

Horses are one of the most loving animals on the planet. Why not spread the love by making your own? This pattern requires a bit more strategic sewing for the mane, but because of the nature of the pieces, any sewing mistakes will be easily hidden.

**Skill Level**
Intermediate

**Size**
Approx 16 inches (40.5 cm) long, 8 inches (20.5 cm) wide and 14 inches (35.5 cm) tall

**Yarn**
Super chunky chenille yarn, Premier Yarns Parfait Chunky, 100% polyester, 131 yds (120 m) and 3.5 oz (100 g) per skein

- Teddy Bear (MC), 2 skeins, 262 yds (240 m) total

- Espresso (C1), ½ skein, approx 66 yds (60 m) total

**Hooks**
US size H-8 (5mm)

**Notions**
Polyester fiberfill
Removable marker
Tapestry needle
Pair of 10mm safety eyes (optional)

**Gauge**
10 sc x 5 rounds = 4 inches (10 cm)

### Abbreviations

**Blo** = back loop only
**C1** = color 1
**Ch(s)** = chain(s)
**Dec** = decrease (crochet 2 sc together)
**Flo** = front loop only
**Inc** = increase (work 2 sc into one stitch)
**MC** = main color
**Sc** = single crochet
**Sl st** = slip stitch
**St(s)** = stitch(es)

## Legs (make 4)

With C1, ch 2 and inc 3 times in the 2nd ch away from hook (6 sts).

**Rnd 1:** Inc in each st (12 sts).

**Rnd 2:** Sc in the blo of each st (12 sts).

**Rnds 3–7:** With MC, sc in each st (12 sts).

Fasten off and leave a 6-inch (15-cm) tail for sewing.

## Tail

With C1, ch 2 and inc 3 times in the 2nd ch away from hook (6 sts).

**Rnds 1–2:** Sc in each st (6 sts).

**Rnds 3–5:** Dec 2 times, inc 2 in the flo (6 sts).

**Rnd 6:** Inc 6 times (12 sts).

**Rnds 7–12:** Sc in each st (12 sts).

**Rnd 13:** (Dec, sc) 4 times (8 sts). Stuff the Tail.

**Rnds 14–16:** Sc in each st (8 sts).

**Rnd 17:** Ch 1. Fold the Tail in half side to side, and sc across through both sides (4 sts) (for more information on sc across both sides, see Gale the Giraffe, page 59).

Fasten off and leave a 6-inch (15-cm) tail for sewing.

## Head

With MC, ch 2 and inc 3 times in the 2nd ch away from hook (6 sts).

**Rnd 1:** Inc 6 times (12 sts).

**Rnd 2:** (Inc, sc) 6 times (18 sts).

**Rnds 3–5:** Sc in each st (18 sts).

**Rnd 6:** Sc 9, inc in the flo of the next 6 sts, sc 3 (24 sts).

**Rnd 7:** Sc 9, (inc, sc) 6 times, sc 3 (30 sts).

**Rnd 8:** Sc in each st (30 sts). If using safety eyes, attach them on this round, 15 sts apart.

Fasten off and leave a 6-inch (15-cm) tail.

## Body

With MC, ch 13. Inc in the 2nd ch from hook, sc in the next 10 chs, and inc 2 times in the last ch. Turn your work clockwise 180 degrees, so that you can work along the opposite side of the ch. Then sc in the next 10 chs, and inc in the last ch (28 sts).

**Rnd 1:** Inc in the first 2 sts, sc 10, inc in the next 4 sts, sc 10, inc in the last 2 sts (36 sts).

**Rnd 2:** (Sc 2, attach Leg with 3 sts, sc 8, attach the next Leg with 3 sts, sc 2) 2 times (36 sts) (for more information on attaching legs, see page 10).

**Rnd 3:** (Sc in the next 2 sts of the Body, sc in the remaining 9 sts of the next Leg, sc in the next 8 sts of the Body, sc in the remaining 9 sts of the next Leg, sc in the next 2 sts of the Body) 2 times (60 sts).

**Rnds 4–12:** Sc in each st (60 sts).

**Rnd 13:** Sc 33, attach the Tail with 4 sts, sc 23 (60 sts).

**Rnd 14:** Sc in each st (60 sts).

**Rnd 15:** (Dec, sc 8) 6 times (54 sts).

**Rnds 16–18:** Sc in each st (54 sts).

**Rnd 19:** (Dec, sc 7) 6 times (48 sts).

**Rnd 20:** (Dec, sc 6) 6 times (42 sts).

**Rnd 21:** Sc 13, (dec, sc 2) 6 times, sc 5 (36 sts). Stuff lightly as you work.

**Rnd 22:** Sc 13, (dec, sc) 6 times, sc 5 (30 sts).

**Rnd 23:** Sc 13, work 6 dec, sc 5 (24 sts).

**Rnd 24:** Sc 15. Place your hook into the flo of the 16th and 17th st (3 sts on hook). Sl st the sts together. Repeat this for the 18th and 15th st, the 19th and 14th st, the 20th and 13th st, and the 21st and 12th st. Inc in the 22nd st (for more information on closing off a body, see Flynn the Fox, page 29). Sc in the remaining 2 sts of this Rnd and the first 11 sts of the next Rnd. This is the new beginning of the Rnd (15 sts). Stuff the Body. Overstuff the Body on Rnds 18–21.

**Rnds 25–26:** Sc in each st (15 sts). This is the Neck portion.

**Rnd 27:** Sc 6, attach the Head with 6 sts, sc 3 (15 sts).

**Rnd 28:** In the next sts of the Neck, sc 4, dec. In the remaining sts of the Head, dec, sc 20, dec. In the remaining sts of the Neck, dec, sc (29 sts).

**Rnd 29:** Sc 13, dec, sc 14 (28 sts).

**Rnd 30:** Sc in each st (28 sts).

**Rnd 31:** (Dec, sc 2) 7 times (21 sts).

**Rnd 32:** Sc in each st (21 sts). Stuff the Head and Neck.

**Rnd 33:** (Dec, sc) 7 times (14 sts).

**Rnd 34:** Dec 7 times (7 sts).

Fasten off and sew the hole closed.

## Mane

With C1, ch 2 and inc 3 times in the 2nd ch away from hook (6 sts).

**Rnd 1:** Sc in each st (6 sts).

**Rnds 3–5:** Dec 2 times. Inc 2 in the flo (6 sts).

**Rnd 6:** (Inc, sc) 3 times (9 sts).

**Rnds 7–9:** Sc in each st (9 sts).

**Rnd 10:** (Inc, sc 2) 3 times (12 sts).

**Rnds 11–12:** Sc in each st (12 sts).

**Rnd 13:** (Inc, sc 3) 3 times (15 sts).

**Rnds 14–18:** Sc in each st (15 sts).

**Rnd 19:** (Dec, sc 3) 3 times (12 sts). Only stuff Rnds 3–17.

**Rnds 20–23:** Sc in each st (12 sts).

**Rnd 24:** (Dec, sc) 4 times (8 sts).

**Rnds 25–26:** Sc in each st (8 sts).

**Rnd 27:** Ch 1. Fold the Mane in half side to side, and sc across through both sides (4 sts) (for more information on sc across both sides, see Gale the Giraffe, page 59).

Fasten off and leave a 6-inch (15-cm) tail for sewing.

## Forelock

With C1, ch 2 and inc 3 times in the 2nd ch away from hook (6 sts).

**Rnd 1:** Sc in each st (6 sts).

**Rnds 3–5:** Dec 2 times. Inc 2 in the flo (6 sts).

**Rnd 6:** Inc 6 times (12 sts).

**Rnds 7–9:** Sc in each st (12 sts). Stuff the Forelock.

**Rnd 10:** Dec 6 times (6 sts).

Fasten off and sew the hole closed. Leave a 6-inch (15-cm) tail for sewing.

## Assembly

Sew Rnd 25 of the Mane to Rnd 28 of the Body. Curve the Mane so that the end lies on the left side of the Neck, and sew Rnd 4 of the Mane to Rnd 19 of the Body (see images 1–4 above). Finally, sew the Forelock to the top of the Head. Weave in all ends.

If you prefer to embroider the eyes instead of using safety eyes, set them 15 sts apart on Rnd 8 of the Head (for more information on sewing eyes onto plushies, see page 13).

# Cara the Chicken

Did you know chickens can dream? If you make your own chicken, it will be able to share dreams with your loved ones as they cuddle in bed. A bit more sewing is required for this chicken, but the sewing is easier with the wings. If you're a beginner, try this pattern to practice your sewing skills!

## Skill Level
Beginner

## Size
Approx 14 inches (35.5 cm) long, 7 inches (18 cm) wide and 10 inches (25.5 cm) tall

## Yarn
Super chunky chenille yarn, Premier Yarns Parfait Chunky, 100% polyester, 131 yds (120 m) and 3.5 oz (100 g) per skein

- Cream (MC), 2 skeins, 262 yds (240 m) total
- Sunshine (C1), ½ skein, approx 66 yds (60 m) total
- Poppy (C2), ⅓ skein, 44 yds (40 m) total

## Hooks
US size H-8 (5mm)

## Notions
Polyester fiberfill
Removable marker used to mark the first stitch of the round
Tapestry needle
Pair of 10mm safety eyes (optional)

## Gauge
10 sc x 5 rounds = 4 inches (10 cm)

### Abbreviations
C1 = color 1
C2 = color 2
Ch(s) = chain(s)
Dec = decrease (crochet 2 sc together)
Flo = front loop only
Inc = increase (work 2 sc into one stitch)
MC = main color
Sc = single crochet
St(s) = stitch(es)

### Pattern Stitches
**Puff Stitch** = Yarn over, insert your hook through the stitch, yarn over and then draw up a loop. Repeat until you have 6 loops on the hook. Yarn over and draw through all 6 loops.

## Legs (make 2)

With C1, ch 2 and inc 3 times in the 2nd ch away from hook (6 sts).

**Rnd 1:** (Inc, sc 2) 2 times (8 sts).

**Rnd 2:** (Inc, sc, inc, Puff st) 2 times (12 sts).

**Rnd 3:** (Dec, sc) 4 times (8 sts).

**Rnd 4:** Ch 1. Place your hook into the 1st and 4th st, and sc across both sides (4 sts) (for more information on sc across both sides, see Gale the Giraffe, page 59).

Fold the Leg flat. Fasten off and leave a 12-inch (30.5-cm) tail. Do not stuff.

## Tail

With MC, ch 2 and inc 3 times in the 2nd ch away from hook (6 sts).

**Rnd 1:** Sc in each st (6 sts).

**Rnd 2:** (Inc, sc 2) 2 times (8 sts).

**Rnd 3:** (Inc, sc 3) 2 times (10 sts).

**Rnd 4:** (Inc, sc 4) 2 times (12 sts). Stuff the Tail.

**Rnd 5:** Sc in each st (12 sts).

Fasten off and leave a 6-inch (15-cm) tail for sewing.

## Beak

With C1, ch 2 and inc 3 times in the 2nd ch away from hook (6 sts).

**Rnd 1:** Sc in each st (6 sts).

**Rnd 2:** (Inc, sc 2) 2 times (8 sts).

Fasten off and leave a 6-inch (15-cm) tail for sewing.

## Wattle

With C2, ch 2 and inc 3 times in the 2nd ch away from hook (6 sts).

**Rnd 1:** (Inc, sc 2) 2 times (8 sts).

**Rnd 2:** Sc 4, Puff st, sc 3 (8 sts).

**Rnd 3:** Sc in each st (8 sts).

**Rnd 4:** Dec 4 times (4 sts).

Fasten off and leave a 6-inch (15-cm) tail for sewing. Do not stuff.

## Wings (make 2)

With MC, ch 2 and inc 3 times in the 2nd ch away from hook (6 sts).

**Rnd 1:** Sc in each st (6 sts).

**Rnd 2:** Sc 2, inc 3 times in the flo, sc (9 sts).

**Rnd 3:** Sc 2, (inc, sc) 3 times, sc (12 sts).

**Rnd 4:** (Inc, sc 2) 4 times (16 sts).

**Rnds 5–6:** Sc in each st (16 sts).

**Rnd 7:** Sc 10, inc 4 times in the flo, sc 2 (20 sts).

**Rnd 8:** Sc 10, (inc, sc) 4 times, sc 2 (24 sts).

**Rnd 9:** Sc in each st (24 sts).

**Rnd 10:** (Dec, sc 2) 6 times (18 sts).

**Rnd 11:** Sc in each st (18 sts).

**Rnd 12:** (Dec, sc) 6 times (12 sts).

**Rnd 13:** Dec 6 times (6 sts).

Fasten off and leave a 6-inch (15-cm) tail for sewing. Fold in half, so the curves of the Wing are visible. Do not stuff.

## Body

With C2, ch 2 and inc 3 times in the 2nd ch away from hook (6 sts).

**Rnd 1:** (Inc, sc 2) 2 times (8 sts).

**Rnd 2:** (Inc, sc, inc, Puff st) 2 times (12 sts).

**Rnd 3:** Sc in each st (12 sts).

**Rnd 4:** (Dec, sc) 4 times (8 sts). Break C2.

**Rnd 5:** With MC, (inc, sc) 4 times (12 sts).

**Rnd 6:** (Inc, sc) 6 times (18 sts).

**Rnd 7:** (Inc, sc 2) 6 times (24 sts).

**Rnd 8:** (Inc, sc 3) 6 times (30 sts).

**Rnd 9:** (Inc, sc 4) 6 times (36 sts).

**Rnds 10–14:** Sc in each st (36 sts).

**Rnd 15:** (Dec, sc 4) 6 times (30 sts).

**Rnd 16:** Sc in each st (30 sts).

**Rnd 17:** (Dec, sc 3) 6 times (24 sts).

**Rnd 18:** (Dec, sc 2) 6 times (18 sts).

**Rnd 19:** Inc 18 times (36 sts).

**Rnd 20:** (Inc, sc 5) 6 times (42 sts).

**Rnds 21–30:** Sc in each st (42 sts). At this time, if using safety eyes, attach them on Rnd 8, 6 sts apart.

**Rnd 31:** (Dec, sc 5) 6 times (36 sts).

**Rnd 32:** (Dec, sc 4) 6 times (30 sts).

**Rnd 33:** Sc 15, attach Leg with 4 sts, sc 2, attach Leg 2 with 4 sts, sc 5 (30 sts) (for more information on attaching legs, see page 10).

**Rnd 34:** (Dec, sc 3) 6 times (24 sts).

**Rnd 35:** (Dec, sc 2) 6 times (18 sts).

**Rnd 36:** (Dec, sc) 6 times (12 sts).

**Rnd 37:** Dec 6 times (6 sts).

Fasten off and sew the hole closed.

## Assembly

Sew each Wing to opposite sides of the Body covering Rnds 21–30. Make sure that the curves of the Wing face the bottom. Sew the Tail to the back of the Body, approximately at Rnd 29. Sew the Beak on Rnds 8–11 of the Head, in the middle. Finally, sew the Wattle to the bottom of the Beak. Weave in all ends.

If you prefer to embroider the eyes instead of using safety eyes, set them 2 sts apart from each side of the Beak sts on Rnd 8 of the Head (for more information on sewing eyes onto plushies, see page 13).

# Wet and Wild

If you're a fan of ocean life, then you're in luck. Friendly dolphins that swim in the cold ocean depths will be within reach with a simple ball or two of yarn. Hippos love the water as well, and the one featured here is a much more manageable size. Penguins love to swim, and the crocheted plushie in this chapter is sure to make a splash! No matter how niche your favorite water-loving animal is, you'll definitely find some cuties in this chapter to get creative with!

In this section, you'll discover some newer techniques to create different sections of the body, but they aren't as hard as you might think. All it includes is slip stitching, which is similar to finishing up a body part by single crocheting it closed (for more information on closing with single crochets, see Flynn the Fox, page 29). As for sewing, this section has the easiest sewing in the entire book! So if you're starting out in crochet with stuffed animals, this will be a great chapter for you.

# Percy the Penguin

It doesn't have to be cold to enjoy penguins! This penguin works up fast and will be next to you in no time. The beak is tiny, but it makes the penguin so cute!

## Skill Level
Beginner

## Size
Approx 6 inches (15 cm) long, 7 inches (18 cm) wide and 10 inches (25.5 cm) tall

## Yarn
Super chunky chenille yarn, Premier Yarns Parfait Chunky, 100% polyester, 131 yds (120 m) and 3.5 oz (100 g) per skein

- Fog (MC), 2 skeins, 262 yds (240 m) total
- Cream (C1), ½ skein, approx 66 yds (60 m) total
- Sunshine (C2), ½ skein, approx 66 yds (60 m) total

## Hooks
US size H-8 (5mm)

## Notions
Polyester fiberfill
Removable marker used to mark the first stitch of the round
Tapestry needle
Pair of 6mm safety eyes (optional)

## Gauge
10 sc x 5 rounds = 4 inches (10 cm)

### Abbreviations

**C1** = color 1

**C2** = color 2

**Ch(s)** = chain(s)

**Dec** = decrease (crochet 2 sc together)

**Inc** = increase (work 2 sc into one stitch)

**MC** = main color

**Sc** = single crochet

**St(s)** = stitch(es)

## Feet (make 2)

With C2, ch 2 and inc 3 times in the 2nd ch away from hook (6 sts).

**Rnd 1:** (Inc, sc 2) 2 times (8 sts).

**Rnd 2:** Sc in each st (8 sts).

**Rnd 3:** Ch 1. Fold the Foot in half, and sc across through both sides (4 sts) (for more information on sc across both sides, see Gale the Giraffe, page 59).

Fasten off and leave a 6-inch (15-cm) for sewing. Do not stuff.

## Tail

With MC, ch 2 and inc 3 times in the 2nd ch away from hook (6 sts).

**Rnds 1–3:** Sc in each st (6 sts).

**Rnd 4:** Ch 1. Fold the Tail in half, and sc across through both sides (3 sts) (for more information on sc across both sides, see Gale the Giraffe, page 59).

Fasten off and leave a 6-inch (15-cm) tail for sewing. Do not stuff.

## Beak

With C2, ch 4. Inc in the 2nd ch from hook, sc, and inc 2 times in the last ch. Turn your work clockwise 180 degrees, so that you can work along the opposite side of the ch. Sc in the next st, and inc in the last st (10 sts).

Fasten off and leave a 6-inch (15-cm) for sewing. Do not stuff.

## Head and Body

With MC, ch 2 and inc 3 times in the 2nd ch away from hook (6 sts).

**Rnd 1:** Inc 6 times (12 sts).

**Rnd 2:** (Inc, sc) 6 times (18 sts).

**Rnd 3:** (Inc, sc 2) 6 times (24 sts).

**Rnd 4:** (Inc, sc 3) 6 times (30 sts).

**Rnds 5–6:** Sc in each st (30 sts).

**Rnd 7:** With MC, sc 4. With C1, sc 3. With MC, sc 2. With C1, sc 3. With MC, sc 18 (30 sts).

**Rnd 8:** With MC, sc 4. With C1, sc 9. With MC, sc 17 (30 sts).

**Rnds 9–10:** With MC, sc 4. With C1, sc 10. With MC, sc 16 (30 sts). If using safety eyes, attach them 5 sts apart on Rnd 10.

**Rnd 11:** With MC, sc 5. With C1, sc 9. With MC, sc 16 (30 sts).

**Rnd 12:** With MC, 3 dec. With C1, 4 dec. With MC, 8 dec (15 sts). Lightly stuff as you work.

**Rnd 13:** With MC, 3 inc. With C1, 4 inc. With MC, 8 inc (30 sts).

**Rnd 14:** With MC, inc, sc 4, inc. With C1, sc 4, inc, sc 4. With MC, (inc, sc 4) 3 times (36 sts).

**Rnds 15–16:** With MC, sc 8. With C1, sc 11. With MC, sc 17 (36 sts).

**Rnd 17:** With MC, sc 9. With C1, sc 10. With MC, sc 17 (36 sts).

**Rnd 18:** With MC, sc 10. With C1, sc 9. With MC, sc 17 (36 sts).

**Rnd 19:** With MC, sc 11. With C1, sc 8. With MC, sc 17 (36 sts).

**Rnd 20:** With MC, sc 12. With C1, sc 7. With MC, sc 17 (36 sts). Break C1.

**Rnds 21–23:** With MC, sc in each st (36 sts).

**Rnd 24:** (Dec, sc 4) 6 times (30 sts). Stuff the Head.

**Rnd 25:** Sc 7. Attach Foot 1, sc 5 and attach Foot 2 to the Body in the same way as Foot 1. Sc 10 (30 sts) (for more information on attaching legs, see page 10).

**Rnd 26:** (Dec, sc 3) 6 times (24 sts).

**Rnd 27:** (Dec, sc 2) 6 times (18 sts). Stuff the Body.

**Rnd 28:** (Dec, sc) 6 times (12 sts).

**Rnd 29:** Dec 6 times (6 sts).

Fasten off and sew the hole closed.

## Wings (make 2)

With MC, ch 2 and inc 3 times in the 2nd ch away from hook (6 sts).

**Rnd 1:** Inc in each st (12 sts).

**Rnds 2–5:** Sc in each st (12 sts).

**Rnd 6:** (Dec, sc) 4 times (8 sts).

**Rnd 7:** Sc in each st (8 sts).

**Rnd 8:** Ch 1. Fold the Wing in half, and sc across through both sides (4 sts) (for more information on sc across both sides, see Gale the Giraffe, page 59).

Fasten off and leave a 6-inch (15-cm) tail for sewing. Do not stuff.

## Assembly

Sew each Wing to the side of the Body, on Rnd 14 of the Body. Sew the Beak to Rnd 10 of the Head, right in the middle. Sew the Tail to the back of the Body, on Rnd 24. Weave in all ends.

If you prefer to embroider the eyes instead of using safety eyes, set them on Rnd 9 of the Head, around the 6th and 12th sts (for more information on sewing eyes onto plushies, see page 13).

# Ollie the Otter

This pattern only requires sewing three pieces together! Because otters have super thick skin, this will make for the perfect teddy bear alternative for loved ones who roughhouse with their toys. Some embroidery for the nose is necessary, but the extra detail gives Ollie so much charm.

**Skill Level**
Intermediate

**Size**
Approx 6 inches (15 cm) long, 7 inches (18 cm) wide and 10 inches (25.5 cm) tall

**Yarn**
Super chunky chenille yarn, Premier Yarns Parfait Chunky, 100% polyester, 131 yds (120 m) and 3.5 oz (100 g) per skein

- Teddy Bear (MC), 2 skeins, 262 yds (240 m) total
- Cream (C1), ½ skein, approx 66 yds (60 m) total
- Chocolate (C2), ¼ skein, approx 33 yds (30 m) total

**Hooks**
US size H-8 (5mm)

**Notions**
Polyester fiberfill
Removable marker
Tapestry needle
Pair of 6mm safety eyes (optional)

**Gauge**
20 sc x 10 rounds = 4 inches (10 cm)

## Abbreviations

**C1** = color 1

**C2** = color 2

**Ch(s)** = chain(s)

**Dec** = decrease (crochet 2 sc together)

**Flo** = front loop only

**Inc** = increase (work 2 sc into one stitch)

**MC** = main color

**Sc** = single crochet

**St(s)** = stitch(es)

## Pattern Stitches

**Puff Stitch** = Yarn over, insert your hook through the st, yarn over and then draw up a loop. Repeat until you have 6 loops on the hook. Yarn over and draw through all 6 loops.

## Arms (make 2)

With MC, ch 2 and inc 3 times in the 2nd ch away from hook (6 sts).

**Rnd 1:** Inc 6 times (12 sts).

**Rnds 2–6:** Sc in each st (12 sts).

Fasten off and leave a 3-inch (7.5-cm) tail. Do not stuff.

## Right Leg

With MC, ch 2 and inc 3 times in the 2nd ch away from hook (6 sts).

**Rnd 1:** Inc 6 times (12 sts).

**Rnd 2:** Sc 4, (Puff st, sc) 3 times, sc 2 (12 sts).

**Rnd 3:** Inc 2 times, sc 2, dec 3 times, sc, inc (12 sts).

**Rnd 4:** Sc in each st (12 sts).

**Rnd 5:** Sc 4, inc 4 times, sc 4 (16 sts).

**Rnd 6:** Sc 4, (inc, sc) 4 times, sc 4 (20 sts).

**Rnd 7:** Sc 17. Leave the remaining 3 sts untouched for accurate Leg attachment to the Body later (17 sts).

Fasten off and leave a 3-inch (7.5-cm) tail. Do not stuff.

## Left Leg

With MC, ch 2 and inc 3 times in the 2nd ch away from hook (6 sts).

**Rnd 1:** Inc 6 times (12 sts).

**Rnd 2:** Sc 2, (sc, Puff st) 3 times, sc 4 (12 sts).

**Rnd 3:** Inc, sc, dec 3 times, sc 2, inc 2 times (12 sts).

**Rnd 4:** Sc in each st (12 sts).

**Rnd 5:** Sc 4, inc 4 times, sc 4 (16 sts).

**Rnd 6:** Sc 4, (sc, inc) 4 times, sc 4 (20 sts).

**Rnd 7:** Sc in each st (20 sts).

Fasten off and leave a 3-inch (7.5-cm) tail. Do not stuff.

## Head

With MC, ch 2 and inc 3 times in the 2nd ch away from hook (6 sts).

**Rnd 1:** With C1, inc 2 times. With MC, inc 4 times (12 sts).

**Rnd 2:** With C1, (sc, inc) 2 times, sc. With MC, inc, (sc, inc) 3 times (18 sts).

**Rnd 3:** With C1, sc 8. With MC, sc 10 (18 sts).

**Rnd 4:** With C1, sc 9. With MC, sc 2. In the flo, inc 6 times. Working in both loops again, sc in the last st (24 sts).

**Rnd 5:** With MC, sc. With C1, sc 8. With MC, sc 2, (inc, sc) 6 times, sc (30 sts). If using safety eyes, attach them on this round, on st 13 and st 27.

**Rnd 6:** With MC, sc 2. With C1, sc 7. With MC, sc 21 (30 sts).

**Rnd 7:** With MC, sc 3. With C1, sc 6. With MC, sc 5. Ch 2 and inc 3 times in the 2nd ch away from hook. This is the first Ear. Sc 14. Ch 2 and inc 3 times in the 2nd ch away from hook. This is the second Ear. Sc 2 (30 sts).

**Rnd 8:** With MC, sc 4. With C1, sc 5. With MC, sc 21 (30 sts). When working around the Rnd, make sure that the Ear is in front of the hook when you work into the next st to allow it to lie flat. Break C1.

**Rnds 9–12:** With MC, sc in each st (30 sts).

**Rnd 13:** (Dec, sc 3) 6 times (24 sts). Stuff the Head.

**Rnd 14:** (Dec, sc 2) 6 times (18 sts).

**Rnd 15:** (Dec, sc) 6 times (12 sts).

**Rnd 16:** Dec 6 times (6 sts).

Fasten off and leave a 12-inch (30.5-cm) tail. Sew the hole closed.

## Body

With C1, ch 13. Inc in the 2nd ch from hook, sc 10, and inc 2 times in the last ch. Turn your work clockwise 180 degrees, so that you can work along the opposite side of the ch. Then sc in the next 10 chs, and inc in the last ch (28 sts).

**Rnd 1:** Inc in the next 2 sts, sc 10, inc in the next 4 sts, sc 10, 2 inc (36 sts).

**Rnd 3:** (Inc, sc 5) 6 times (42 sts).

**Rnd 4:** Sc 6, attach Arm with 3 sts, sc 4, attach Left Leg with 6 sts, sc 5, attach Right Leg with 6 sts, sc 4, attach Arm with 3 sts, sc 5 (42 sts) (for more information on attaching limbs to a body, see page 10).

**Rnd 5:** With C1, sc in the next 6 sts of the Body. With MC, sc in the remaining 9 sts of the Arm. With C1, sc in the next 4 sts of the Body. With MC, sc in the remaining 14 sts of the Left Leg. With C1, sc in the next 5 sts of the Body. With MC, sc in the remaining 14 sts of the Right Leg. With C1, sc in the next 4 sts of the Body. With MC, sc in the remaining 9 sts of the Arm. Sc in the remaining 5 sts of the Body (70 sts). Break C1.

**Rnd 6:** With MC, sc 6, dec, sc 3, dec, sc 47, dec, sc 3, dec, sc 3 (66 sts).

**Rnds 7–8:** Sc in each st (6 sts).

**Rnd 9:** (Dec, sc 4) 2 times, sc 13, (dec, sc 4) 3 times, sc 17, dec, sc 4 (60 sts).

**Rnd 10:** (Dec, sc 3) 2 times, sc 13, (dec, sc 3) 3 times, sc 17, dec, sc 3 (54 sts).

**Rnds 11–12:** Sc in each st (54 sts).

**Rnd 13:** (Dec, sc 2) 2 times, sc 13, (dec, sc 2) 3 times, sc 17, dec, sc 2 (48 sts).

**Rnd 14:** Sc in each st (48 sts).

**Rnd 15:** (Dec, sc) 2 times, sc 13, (dec, sc) 3 times, sc 17, dec, sc (42 sts).

**Rnd 16:** Sc in each st (42 sts).

**Rnd 17:** Dec 2 times, sc 13, dec 3 times, sc 17, dec (36 sts).

**Rnd 18:** (Dec, sc 4) 6 times (30 sts).

**Rnd 19:** (Dec, sc 3) 6 times (24 sts).

**Rnd 20:** (Dec, sc 2) 6 times (18 sts).

**Rnd 21:** (Dec, sc) 6 times (12 sts).

**Rnd 22:** Dec 6 times (6 sts).

Fasten off and sew the hole closed.

## Tail

With MC, ch 2 and inc 3 times in the 2nd ch away from hook (6 sts).

**Rnd 1:** Sc in each st (6 sts).

**Rnd 2:** (Inc, sc) 3 times (9 sts).

**Rnds 3–5:** Sc in each st (9 sts).

**Rnd 6:** (Inc, sc 2) 3 times (12 sts). Stuff the Tail.

**Rnds 7–10:** Sc in each st (12 sts).

Fasten off and leave a 6-inch (15-cm) tail for sewing.

## Assembly

Sew the Head on top of the Body, right between the Arms. Sew the Tail to the bottom of the Body on Rnds 8–10. With C2, embroider a V-shaped nose covering Rnds 1–2 of the face (see images 1–4 above). Weave in all ends. With C2, embroider a large circle (identical to embroidering eyes), covering Rnds 1-2 of the Feet (for more information on embroidering this shape, refer to page 13).

If you prefer to embroider the eyes instead of using safety eyes, set them on Rnd 5 of the Head on st 13 and st 27 (for more information on embroidering eyes, see page 13).

# Daisy the Dolphin

Although dolphins are surprisingly slow swimmers, this simple pattern works up fast! In this pattern, I use a special technique to make sure the colors of the dolphin's belly stay aligned and straight with the body. It looks jagged or slanted at first, but as you continue to build round by round, the jaggedness creates a unique look!

## Skill Level
Beginner

## Size
Approx 12 inches (30.5 cm) long, 5 inches (12.5 cm) wide and 5 inches (12.5 cm) tall

## Yarn
Super chunky chenille yarn, Premier Yarns Parfait Chunky, 100% polyester, 131 yds (120 m) and 3.5 oz (100 g) per skein

- Pale Blue (MC), 2 skeins, 262 yds (240 m) total
- Cream (C1), ½ skein, approx 66 yds (60 m) total

## Hooks
US size H-8 (5mm)

## Notions
Polyester fiberfill
Removable marker to mark the first st of the round
Tapestry needle
Pair of 6mm safety eyes (optional)

## Gauge
10 sc x 5 rounds = 4 inches (10 cm)

### Abbreviations
C1 = color 1

Ch(s) = chain(s)

Dec = decrease (crochet 2 sc together)

Flo = front loop only

Inc = increase (work 2 sc into one stitch)

MC = main color

Sc = single crochet

Sl st = slip stitch

St(s) = stitch(es)

## Flippers (make 2)

With MC, ch 2 and inc 3 times in the 2nd ch away from hook (6 sts).

**Rnd 1:** Inc in each st (12 sts).

**Rnd 2:** (Inc, sc 2) 4 times (16 sts).

**Rnds 3–4:** Sc in each st (16 sts).

**Rnd 5:** Ch 1. Fold the Flipper in half side to side, and sc across through both sides (8 sts) (for more information on sc across both sides, see Gale the Giraffe, page 59).

Fasten off and leave a 6-inch (15-cm) tail for sewing.

## Body and Tail

With MC, ch 2 and inc 3 times in the 2nd ch away from hook (6 sts).

**Rnd 1:** With MC, inc 4. With C1, inc 2 (12 sts).

**Rnd 2:** With MC, (sc, inc) 4 times. With C1, (sc, inc) 2 times (18 sts).

**Rnd 3:** With MC, sc 12. With C1, sc 6 (18 sts).

**Rnd 4:** With C1, sc. With MC, sc 11. With C1, sc 6 (18 sts).

**Rnd 5:** With C1, sc. With MC, sc 3. In the flo, inc 6 times. In both loops, sc 3. With C1, sc 5 (24 sts).

**Rnd 6:** With C1, sc 2. With MC, sc 2, (inc, sc) 6 times, sc 3. With C1, sc 5 (30 sts).

**Rnd 7:** With C1, sc 2. With MC, sc 2, (inc, sc 2) 6 times, sc 4. With C1, sc 4 (36 sts).

**Rnd 8:** With C1, sc 3. With MC, sc 29. With C1, sc 4 (36 sts). If using safety eyes, attach them on this round, 22 sts apart.

**Rnd 9:** With C1, sc 3. With MC, sc 2, (inc, sc 5) 4 times, inc, sc 2. With C1, sc 3, inc (42 sts).

**Rnd 10:** With C1, sc 4. With MC, sc 33. With C1, sc 5 (42 sts).

**Rnd 11:** With C1, sc 5. With MC, sc 32. With C1, sc 5 (42 sts).

**Rnd 12:** With C1, sc 5. With MC, sc 33. With C1, sc 4 (42 sts).

**Rnd 13:** With C1, sc 6. With MC, sc 33. With C1, sc 3 (42 sts).

**Rnd 14:** With C1, sc 7. With MC, sc 33. With C1, sc 2 (42 sts).

**Rnd 15:** With C1, sc 7. With MC, sc 32. With C1, sc 3 (42 sts).

**Rnd 16:** With C1, sc 8. With MC, sc 32. With C1, sc 2 (42 sts).

**Rnd 17:** With C1, sc 9. With MC, sc 32. With C1, sc (42 sts).

**Rnd 18:** With C1, sc 9. With MC, sc 33 (42 sts).

**Rnd 19:** With C1, sc 10. With MC, sc 32 (42 sts).

**Rnd 20:** With C1, sc 10. With MC, sc 32 (42 sts).

**Rnd 21:** With MC, sc. With C1, sc 4, dec, sc 4. With MC, sc, (dec, sc 5) 4 times, dec (36 sts).

**Rnd 22:** With MC, sc. With C1, sc 9. With MC, sc 26 (36 sts).

**Rnd 23:** With MC, sc 2. With C1, sc 9. With MC, sc 2, (dec, sc 2) 5 times, dec, sc (30 sts).

**Rnd 24:** With MC, sc 2. With C1, sc 9. With MC, sc 19 (30 sts).

**Rnd 25:** With MC, sc 3. With C1, sc 9. With MC, sc, (dec, sc) 5 times, dec (24 sts).

**Rnd 26:** With MC, sc 3. With C1, sc 9. With MC, sc 12 (24 sts).

**Rnd 27:** With MC, sc 4. With C1, sc 9. With MC, sc, dec 5 times (19 sts).

**Rnd 28:** With MC, dec, sc 2. With C1, sc 9. With MC, sc 6 (18 sts).

**Rnd 29:** With MC, sc 4. With C1, sc 9. With MC, sc 5 (18 sts).

**Rnds 30–31:** With MC, sc 5. With C1, sc 9. With MC, sc 4 (18 sts).

**Rnd 32:** With MC, dec, sc 4. With C1, sc 3, dec, sc 4. With MC, sc 3 (16 sts). Stuff the Body.

**Rnd 33:** With MC, sc 5. With C1, sc 8. With MC, sc 3 (16 sts).

**Rnd 34:** With MC, dec, sc 2, dec, sc. With C1, sc, dec, sc 2, dec, sc. With MC, sc (12 sts).

**Rnd 35:** With MC, sc 5. With C1, sc 6. With MC, sc (12 sts).

**Rnd 36:** With MC, (dec, sc) 2 times. With C1, dec, sc, dec. With MC, sc (8 sts). Break C1.

**Rnd 37:** With MC, inc 8 times in the flo (16 sts).

**Rnd 38:** (Inc, sc) 8 times (24 sts).

**Rnds 39–42:** Sc in each st (24 sts). Stuff the Tail.

**Rnd 43:** Fold the Tail in half side to side, and sl st across through both sides (12 sts) (for more information on how to work across both sides, see Gale the Giraffe, page 59).

Fasten off and weave in the remaining ends.

## Fin

With MC, ch 2 and inc 3 times in the 2nd ch away from hook (6 sts).

**Rnd 1:** Sc in each st (6 sts).

**Rnd 2:** (Inc, sc) 3 times (9 sts).

**Rnd 3:** Sc 3, inc 3 times in the flo, sc 3 (12 sts).

**Rnd 4:** Sc in each st (12 sts).

Fasten off and leave a 6-inch (15-cm) tail for sewing. Do not stuff.

## Assembly

Sew each Flipper on opposite sides of the Body, aligning each on the line where C1 and MC meet, on Rnds 13–20 of the Body. Sew the Fin on top of the Body, aligning it in the top middle on Rnds 13–16 of the Body. Weave in all ends.

If you prefer to embroider the eyes instead of using safety eyes, set them 22 sts apart on Rnd 9 of the Head (for more information on sewing eyes onto plushies, see page 13).

# Opal the Octopus

Did you know an octopus has three hearts? Opal the octopus will definitely capture yours next! The most tedious part of making the octopus is making every leg. However, it's also satisfying seeing each leg get finished. Connecting all of them to make the final plushie brings it to life before your eyes.

## Skill Level
Beginner

## Size
Approx 14 inches (36 cm) long, 7 inches (18 cm) wide and 10 inches (25.5 cm) tall

## Yarn
Super chunky chenille yarn, Premier Yarns Parfait Chunky, 100% polyester, 131 yds (120 m) and 3.5 oz (100 g) per skein

- Iris (MC), 2 skeins, 262 yds (240 m) total
- White (C1), ½ skein, approx 66 yds (60 m) total

## Hooks
US size H-8 (5mm)

## Notions
Polyester fiberfill
Removable marker used to mark the first stitch of the round
Tapestry needle
Pair of 6mm safety eyes (optional)

## Gauge
10 sc x 5 rounds = 4 inches (10 cm)

### Abbreviations

**C1** = color 1

**Ch(s)** = chain(s)

**Dec** = decrease (crochet 2 sc together)

**Inc** = increase (work 2 sc into one stitch)

**MC** = main color

**Sc** = single crochet

**St(s)** = stitch(es)

### Pattern Stitches

**Puff Stitch** = Yarn over, insert your hook through the st, yarn over and then draw up a loop. Repeat until you have 6 loops on the hook. Yarn over and draw through all 6 loops.

## Legs (make 8)

With MC, ch 2 and inc 2 times in the 2nd ch away from hook (4 sts).

**Rnd 1:** Sc in each st (4 sts).

**Rnd 2:** (Inc, sc) 2 times (6 sts).

**Rnd 3:** Sc in each st (6 sts).

**Rnd 4:** With C1, sc. With MC, sc 5 (6 sts).

**Rnd 5:** With C1, inc, sc. With MC, sc, inc, sc 2 (8 sts).

**Rnd 6:** With C1, sc, Puff st, sc. With MC, sc 5 (8 sts).

**Rnds 7–8:** With MC, sc. With C1, sc 3. With MC, sc 4 (8 sts).

**Rnd 9:** With MC, sc 2. With C1, sc 3. With MC, sc 3 (8 sts).

**Rnd 10:** With MC, sc 2. With C1, Puff st, sc, Puff st. With MC, sc 3 (8 sts).

**Rnds 11–12:** With MC, sc 3. With C1, sc 3. With MC, sc 2 (8 sts).

**Rnd 13:** With MC, sc 4. With C1, sc 3. With MC, sc (8 sts).

**Rnd 14:** With MC, sc 4. With C1, sc, Puff st, sc. With MC, sc (8 sts).

**Rnds 15–16:** With MC, sc 5. With C1, sc 3 (8 sts).

**Rnd 17:** With MC, sc 6. With C1, sc 2 (8 sts).

**Rnd 18:** With C1, sc. With MC, sc 5. With C1, sc 2 (8 sts).

**Rnd 19:** With C1, sc. With MC, sc 6. With C1, Puff st (8 sts).

**Rnd 20:** With C1, sc, Puff st. With MC, sc 5. With C1, sc (8 sts).

**Rnds 21–22:** With C1, sc 2. With MC, sc 6 (8 sts).

Fasten off and leave a 3-inch (7.5-cm) tail.

## Body

With C1, ch 2 and inc 4 times in the 2nd ch away from hook (8 sts).

**Rnd 1:** Inc 8 times (16 sts).

**Rnd 2:** (Inc, sc) 8 times (24 sts).

**Rnd 3:** (Inc, sc 2) 8 times (32 sts).

**Rnd 4:** (With C1, attach Leg with 2 sts. With MC, sc 2) 8 times (32 sts) (for more information on attaching legs to a body, see page 10). Break C1.

**Rnd 7:** (Sc in the remaining 6 sts of the Leg, sc in the next 2 sts of the Body) 8 times (64 sts).

**Rnds 8–19:** Sc in each st (64 sts).

**Rnd 20:** (Dec, sc 6) 8 times (56 sts). Stuff the Legs.

**Rnd 21:** Sc in each st (56 sts).

**Rnd 22:** (Dec, sc 5) 8 times (48 sts).

**Rnd 23:** (Dec, sc 6) 6 times (42 sts).

**Rnd 24:** (Dec, sc 5) 6 times (36 sts). Stuff the Body.

**Rnd 25:** (Dec, sc 4) 6 times (30 sts).

**Rnd 26:** (Dec, sc 3) 6 times (24 sts).

**Rnd 27:** (Dec, sc 2) 6 times (18 sts).

**Rnd 28:** (Dec, sc) 6 times (12 sts).

**Rnd 29:** Dec 6 times (6 sts).

Fasten off and sew the hole closed.

## Eyes (make 2)

With MC, ch 2 and inc 3 times in the 2nd ch away from hook (6 sts). If using safety eyes, attach them on this round, in the center.

**Rnd 1:** (Inc, sc) 3 times (9 sts).

**Rnd 2:** Sc in each st (9 sts).

Fasten off and leave an 8-inch (20.5-cm) tail for sewing.

## Assembly

Sew the Eyes to the front of the Body on Rnds 10–12, 20 sts apart. Weave in all ends.

If you prefer to embroider the eyes instead of using safety eyes, set them on Rnd 1 of the Eyes (for more information on embroidering eyes, see page 13).

# Fern the Frog

There are more than 6,000 species of frogs, so mix and match colors to create as many different species as you'd like! This frog pattern (unlike a lot of other frog crochet patterns) is on the anatomical side. Making the tiny toes of each foot is the best part!

**Skill Level**
Intermediate

**Size**
Approx 14 inches (3.5 cm) long, 7 inches (18 cm) wide and 10 inches (25.5 cm) tall

**Yarn**
Super chunky chenille yarn, Premier Yarns Parfait Chunky, 100% polyester, 131 yds (120 m) and 3.5 oz (100 g) per skein

- Lime Green (MC), 2 skeins, 262 yds (240 m) total
- Iris (C1), ½ skein, approx 66 yds (60 m) total

**Hooks**
US size H-8 (5mm)

**Notions**
Polyester fiberfill
Removable marker used to mark the first stitch of the round
Tapestry needle
Pair of 10mm safety eyes (optional)

**Gauge**
10 sc x 5 rounds = 4 inches (10 cm)

## Abbreviations

**C1** = color 1

**Ch(s)** = chain(s)

**Dec** = decrease (crochet 2 sc together)

**Flo** = front loop only

**Inc** = increase (work 2 sc into one stitch)

**MC** = main color

**Sc** = single crochet

**Sl st** = slip stitch

**St(s)** = stitch(es)

## Pattern Stitches

**Puff Stitch** = Yarn over, insert your hook through the st, yarn over and then draw up a loop. Repeat until you have 4 loops on the hook. Yarn over and draw through all 4 loops.

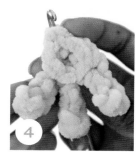

## Back Legs (make 2)

With MC, ch 2 and inc 3 times in the 2nd ch away from hook (6 sts).

**Rnd 1:** (Sc, ch 4 and Puff st in the 2nd ch from hook. Sl st in the remaining 2 chs) 3 times, sc 3 (15 sts). See image 1 above which shows Rnd 1 complete.

**Rnd 2:** Sc in each sc only (Do not sc into the chs we worked in from Rnd 1; those are the frog's toes) (6 sts) (see images 2–4 above).

**Rnds 3–6:** Sc in each st (6 sts).

**Rnd 7:** (Inc, sc) 3 times (9 sts).

**Rnd 8:** Sc in each st (9 sts).

**Rnd 9:** (Inc, sc 2) 3 times (12 sts).

**Rnds 10–12:** Dec 3 times. In the flo, inc 4 times. In both loops, dec (12 sts).

**Rnds 13–14:** Sc in each st (12 sts). Stuff the Legs.

**Rnd 15:** Dec 6 times (6 sts).

Fasten off and leave a 6-inch (15-cm) tail for sewing. Sew the hole closed.

## Front Legs (make 2)

With MC, ch 2 and inc 3 times in the 2nd ch away from hook (6 sts).

**Rnd 1:** Sc, (sc, ch 4 and Puff st in the 2nd ch from hook. Sl st in the remaining 2 chs) 3 times, sc 2 (15 sts).

**Rnd 2:** Sc in each sc only (6 sts) (do not sc into the chs we worked in from Rnd 1; those are the toes).

**Rnd 3:** Sc in each st (6 sts).

**Rnds 4–6:** Dec 1 time, inc 2 times in the flo, dec 1 time (6 sts).

**Rnd 7:** Inc 6 times (12 sts). Stuff the Legs.

**Rnds 8–9:** Sc in each st (12 sts).

**Rnd 10:** Dec 6 times (6 sts).

Fasten off and leave a 6-inch (15-cm) tail for sewing. Sew the hole closed.

## Eyes (make 2)

With MC, ch 2 and inc 3 times in the 2nd ch away from hook (6 sts).

**Rnd 1:** Inc 6 times (12 sts).

**Rnd 2:** Sc in each st (12 sts).

Fasten off and leave a 3-inch (7.5-cm) tail. Do not stuff.

## Head and Body

**Rnd 1:** With MC, ch 2 and inc 3 times in the 2nd ch away from hook (6 sts).

**Rnd 2:** Inc 6 times (12 sts).

**Rnd 3:** (Sc 2, attach Eye with 4 sts) 2 times (12 sts) (for more information on attaching body parts, see page 10).

**Rnd 4:** Sc in the next 2 sts of the Head, sc in the remaining 8 sts of the Eye, inc in the next 2 sts of the Head, sc in the remaining 8 sts of the Eye (22 sts).

**Rnd 5:** Sc 8, (inc, sc) 4 times, sc 6 (26 sts).

**Rnd 6:** Sc 13, inc 4 times, sc 5, (inc, sc) 2 times (32 sts).

**Rnd 7:** (Inc, sc) 4 times, sc 24 (36 sts).

**Rnd 8:** (Inc, sc 2) 4 times, sc 6, dec 4 times, sc 10 (36 sts).

**Rnd 9:** Sc 33, inc, sc 2 (37 sts).

**Rnd 10:** (Inc, sc 2) 5 times, (dec, sc) 6 times, sc 4 (36 sts).

**Rnd 11:** With MC, sc 22. With C1, sc 9. With MC, sc 5 (36 sts).

**Rnds 12–13:** With MC, sc 21. With C1, sc 12. With MC, sc 3 (36 sts).

**Rnd 14:** With MC, (inc, sc 5) 3 times, inc, sc. With C1, sc 4, inc, sc 5, inc, sc 3. With MC, sc 2 (42 sts).

**Rnd 15:** With MC, sc 24. With C1, sc 17. With MC, sc (42 sts).

**Rnds 16–17:** With MC, sc 24. With C1, sc 18 (42 sts).

**Rnd 18:** With C1, sc. With MC, sc 23. With C1, sc 18 (42 sts).

**Rnd 19:** With C1, sc 2. With MC, sc 22. With C1, sc 18 (42 sts). At this time, if using safety eyes, attach them on Rnd 2 of the Eyes, on the side of each Eye.

**Rnd 20:** With C1, sc 2. With MC, sc 23. With C1, sc 17 (42 sts).

**Rnd 21:** With C1, sc 2. With MC, sc 24. With C1, sc 16 (42 sts).

**Rnd 22:** With C1, sc 2. With MC, sc 25. With C1, sc 15 (42 sts). Stuff the Head.

**Rnd 23:** With C1, sc 2. With MC, sc 26. With C1, sc 14 (42 sts).

**Rnd 24:** With C1, sc 2. With MC, sc 27. With C1, sc 13 (42 sts).

**Rnd 25:** With C1, dec. With MC, sc 5, (dec, sc 5) 3 times, dec. With C1, sc 5, dec, sc 5 (36 sts).

**Rnd 26:** With C1, sc. With MC, sc 25. With C1, sc 10 (36 sts).

**Rnd 27:** With C1, dec. With MC, sc 4, (dec, sc 4) 3 times, dec, sc. With C1, sc 3, dec, sc 4 (30 sts).

**Rnd 28:** With C1, sc. With MC, sc 22. With C1, sc 7 (30 sts). Stuff the Body.

**Rnd 29:** With MC, (dec, sc 3) 4 times, dec, sc 2. With C1, sc, dec, sc 3 (24 sts). Break C1.

**Rnd 30:** With MC, (dec, sc 2) 6 times (18 sts).

**Rnd 31:** (Dec, sc) 6 times (12 sts).

**Rnd 32:** Dec 6 times (6 sts).

Fasten off and sew the hole closed.

## Assembly

Sew the Back Legs to the back of the Body, aligning Rnds 13–15 of each Back Leg to Rnds 25–30 of the Body. (Note: Rnd 32 is the back of the Body, while Rnd 1 is the front of the Head.) Sew the Front Legs to the front of the Body, aligning Rnds 8–10 of the Legs to Rnds 16–20 of the Body. Weave in all ends.

If you prefer to embroider the eyes instead of using safety eyes, set them on Rnd 1 of the Eyes, positioning them on the side of each Eye (for more information on embroidering eyes, see page 13).

# Heidi the Hippo

This hippo will use up a lot of yarn—they are one of the largest mammals on the planet, after all! This pattern doesn't use too many techniques, so you'll be able to coast through it with ease. Hippos come in a range of colors, so mix and match to make a multitude, from a regular gray hippo to a cartoon-like purple hippo—to even a muddy hippo!

## Skill Level
Beginner

## Size
Approx 14 inches (35.5 cm) long, 7 inches (18 cm) wide and 10 inches (25.5 cm) tall

## Yarn
Super chunky chenille yarn, Premier Yarns Parfait Chunky, 100% polyester, 131 yds (120 m) and 3.5 oz (100 g) per skein

- Lilac (MC), 2 skeins, 262 yds (240 m) total
- Iris (C1), ½ skein, approx 66 yds (60 m) total

## Hooks
US size H-8 (5mm)

## Notions
Polyester fiberfill
Removable marker used to mark the first stitch of the round
Tapestry needle
Pair of 6mm safety eyes (optional)

## Gauge
10 sc x 5 rounds = 4 inches (10 cm)

### Abbreviations
**Blo** = back loop only
**C1** = color 1
**Ch(s)** = chain(s)
**Dec** = decrease (crochet 2 sc together)
**Flo** = front loop only
**Inc** = increase (work 2 sc into one stitch)
**MC** = main color
**Sc** = single crochet
**St(s)** = stitch(es)

### Pattern Stitches
**Puff Stitch** = Yarn over, insert your hook through the st, yarn over and then draw up a loop. Repeat until you have 6 loops on the hook. Yarn over and draw through all 6 loops.

## Legs (make 4)

With C1, ch 2 and inc 3 times in the 2nd ch away from hook (6 sts).

**Rnd 1:** Inc in each st (12 sts).

**Rnd 2:** Sc in the blo of each st (12 sts). Break C1.

**Rnd 3:** With MC, sc in the blo of each st (12 sts).

**Rnd 4:** Sc in each st (12 sts).

Fasten off and leave a 6-inch (15-cm) tail.

## Tail

With MC, ch 6. Puff st in the 2nd ch from hook and sc in the remaining 4 chs. Fasten off and leave a 6-inch (15-cm) tail.

## Body

With MC, ch 10. Inc in the 2nd ch from hook, sc in the next 7 chs, and inc 2 times in the last ch. Turn your work clockwise 180 degrees, so that you can work along the opposite side of the ch. Then, sc in the next 7 chs, and inc in the last ch (22 sts).

**Rnd 1:** Inc in the first 2 sts, sc 7, inc in the next 4 sts, sc 7, inc in the last 2 sts (30 sts).

**Rnd 2:** (Sc 2, attach Leg with 3 sts, sc 5, attach the next Leg with 3 sts, sc 2) 2 times (30 sts) (for more information on attaching legs, see page 10).

**Rnd 3:** (Sc in the first 2 sts of the Body, sc in the remaining 9 sts of the Leg, sc in the next 5 sts of the Body, sc in the remaining 9 sts of the next Leg, sc in the next 2 sts of the Body) 2 times (54 sts).

**Rnd 4:** (Inc, sc 8) 6 times (60 sts).

**Rnds 5–10:** Sc in each st (60 sts).

**Rnd 11:** (Dec, sc 8) 6 times (54 sts).

**Rnds 12–14:** Sc in each st (54 sts). Lightly stuff the Body as you work.

**Rnd 15:** (Dec, sc 7) 6 times (48 sts).

**Rnds 16–17:** Sc in each st (48 sts). Place a removable marker on Rnd 17.

**Rnd 18:** (Dec, sc 6) 6 times (42 sts).

**Rnd 19:** Sc in each st (42 sts).

**Rnd 20:** (Dec, sc 5) 6 times (36 sts). Stuff the Body.

**Rnd 21:** (Dec, sc 4) 6 times (30 sts).

**Rnd 22:** (Dec, sc 3) 6 times (24 sts).

**Rnd 23:** (Dec, sc 2) 6 times (18 sts).

**Rnd 24:** (Dec, sc) 6 times (12 sts).

**Rnd 25:** Dec 6 times (6 sts).

Fasten off and sew the hole closed.

## Ears (make 2)

With MC, ch 2 and inc 3 times in the 2nd ch away from hook (6 sts).

Fasten off and leave a 3-inch (7.5-cm) tail.

## Head

With MC, ch 2 and inc 4 times in the 2nd ch away from hook (8 sts).

**Rnd 1:** Inc 8 times (16 sts).

**Rnd 2:** (Inc, sc) 8 times (24 sts).

**Rnd 3:** Sc 8, Puff st, sc 7, Puff st, sc 7 (24 sts).

**Rnd 4:** (Inc, sc 3) 6 times (30 sts).

**Rnd 5:** (Inc, sc 4) 6 times (36 sts).

**Rnds 6–9:** Sc in each st (36 sts).

**Rnd 10:** (Dec, sc 4) 6 times (30 sts).

**Rnd 11:** Sc in each st (30 sts).

**Rnd 12:** (Dec, sc 3) 6 times (24 sts).

**Rnd 13:** In the flo, (inc, sc 3) 6 times (30 sts). If using safety eyes, attach them 11 sts apart on this Rnd.

**Rnds 14–16:** Sc in each st (30 sts).

**Rnd 17:** Sc 17, attach Ear 1. When attaching the Ear, make sure that the right side of the Head and the right side of the Ear are touching each other. Sc 6, attach Ear 2 in the same manner as Ear 1, sc 5 (30 sts).

**Rnd 18:** (Dec, sc 3) 6 times (24 sts).

**Rnd 19:** (Dec, sc 2) 6 times (18 sts).

**Rnd 20:** (Dec, sc) 6 times (12 sts).

**Rnd 21:** Dec 6 times (6 sts).

Fasten off and leave an 8-inch (20.5-cm) tail. Sew the hole closed.

## Assembly

Sew the Head to the front of the Body on Rnds 15–20. Sew the Tail to the back of the Body on Rnd 11. Weave in all ends.

If you prefer to embroider the eyes instead of using safety eyes, set them 11 sts apart on Rnd 13 of the Head (for more information on embroidering eyes, see page 13).

# Theodore the Turtle

If you've seen a turtle before, you know that their speed isn't . . . speedy per se. Although turtles are traditionally slow, this turtle can be worked up in a couple of hours! Soon, you'll have your own Theodore to love.

## Skill Level
Intermediate

## Size
Approx 8 inches (20.5 cm) long, 9 inches (23 cm) wide and 8 inches (20.5 cm) tall

## Yarn
Super chunky chenille yarn, Premier Yarns Parfait Chunky, 100% polyester, 131 yds (120 m) and 3.5 oz (100 g) per skein

- Emerald (MC), 2 skeins, 262 yds (240 m) total
- Lime Green (C1), ½ skein, approx 66 yds (60 m) total
- Seashell (C2), ½ skein, approx 66 yds (60 m) total

## Hooks
US size H-8 (5mm)

## Notions
Polyester fiberfill
Removable marker used to mark the first stitch of the round
Tapestry needle
Pair of 10mm safety eyes (optional)

## Gauge
10 sc x 5 rounds = 4 inches (10 cm)

### Abbreviations
**Blo** = back loop only
**C1** = color 1
**C2** = color 2
**Ch(s)** = chain(s)
**Dec** = decrease (crochet 2 sc together)
**Flo** = front loop only
**Inc** = increase (work 2 sc into one stitch)
**MC** = main color
**Sc** = single crochet
**St(s)** = stitch(es)

   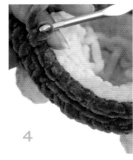

## Legs (make 4)

With C1, ch 2 and inc 3 times in the 2nd ch away from hook (6 sts).

**Rnd 1:** Inc in each st (12 sts).

**Rnd 2:** Sc in the blo each st (12 sts).

**Rnds 3–5:** With MC, sc in each st (12 sts).

Fasten off and leave a 6-inch (15-cm) tail.

## Belly

With C2, ch 2 and inc 3 times in the 2nd ch away from hook (6 sts).

**Rnd 1:** Inc in each st (12 sts).

**Rnd 2:** (Inc, sc) 6 times (18 sts).

**Rnd 3:** (Inc, sc 2) 6 times (24 sts).

**Rnd 4:** (Inc, sc 3) 6 times (30 sts).

**Rnd 5:** Sc in the next 4 sts, attach Leg 1 with 4 sts, (sc 2, attach the next Leg with 4 sts) 3 times, sc in the last 4 sts (30 sts) (for more information on attaching legs, see page 10).

**Rnd 6:** With C2, sc in the next 4 sts of the Body. (With C1, sc in the remaining 8 sts of the Leg. With C2, sc in the next 2 sts of the Body) 4 times. With C2, sc in the last 2 sts of the Body (46 sts). Break C1.

**Rnd 7:** With C2, (inc in the flo, sc 5 in the flo) 7 times, inc, sc 3 (54 sts).

**Rnds 8–9:** With C2, sc in each st (54 sts). Break C2.

**Rnd 10:** We will now start the shell. With MC, sc in the flo of each st (54 sts).

**Rnds 11–13:** Sc in each st (54 sts). Stuff the Legs.

**Rnd 14:** [Place your hook in the blo of the next st and the blo of Rnd 10 (see images 1–2 above). Sc both sts together (image 3)] 54 times (54 sts). Start to lightly stuff the Body as you go.

**Rnds 15–18:** Sc in each st (54 sts).

**Rnd 19:** (Dec, sc 7) 6 times (48 sts).

**Rnd 20:** Sc in each st (48 sts).

**Rnd 21:** (Dec, sc 6) 6 times (42 sts).

**Rnd 22:** Sc in each st (42 sts).

**Rnd 23:** (Dec, sc 5) 6 times (36 sts).

**Rnd 24:** Sc in each st (36 sts).

**Rnd 25:** (Dec in the blo, sc 4 in the blo) 6 times (30 sts).

**Rnd 26:** (Dec, sc 3) 6 times (24 sts). Continue stuffing the Body.

**Rnd 27:** (Dec, sc 2) 6 times (18 sts).

**Rnd 28:** (Dec, sc) 6 times (12 sts).

**Rnd 29:** Dec 6 times (6 sts).

Fasten off and finish stuffing the Body. Sew the hole closed.

## Head

With C1, ch 2 and inc 3 times in the 2nd ch away from hook (6 sts).

**Rnd 1:** Inc 6 times (12 sts).

**Rnd 2:** (Inc, sc) 6 times (18 sts).

**Row 3:** (Inc, sc 2) 6 times (24 sts).

**Rnds 4–7:** Sc in each st (24 sts). Stuff the top of the Head. On Rnd 5, if using safety eyes, attach them on this round, 5 sts apart.

**Rnd 8:** (Dec, sc 2) 6 times (18 sts). Place a removable marker on this Rnd.

**Rnd 9:** (Dec, sc) 6 times (12 sts). Only stuff the Neck on Rnds 1–8.

**Rnds 10–15:** Sc in each st (12 sts).

Fasten off and leave a 10-inch (25.5-cm) tail.

## Tail

With C1, ch 2 and inc 3 times in the 2nd ch away from hook (6 sts).

**Rnd 1:** (Inc, sc) 3 times (9 sts).

**Rnds 2–4:** Sc in each st (9 sts).

Fasten off and leave a 6-inch (15-cm) tail. Do not stuff.

## Assembly

Sew Rnd 15 of the Head to the front of the Body, on Rnd 7 of the Belly. Sew Rnd 7 of the back of the Head to Rnd 12 of the shell. Sew the Tail to the opposite side of the Belly, on Rnd 7. Weave in all ends.

If you prefer to embroider the eyes instead of using safety eyes, set them on Rnd 7 of the Head, 5 sts apart (for more information on embroidering eyes, see page 13).

# Mythological Creatures

Fairy tales are the stories that never get old—so mythological creatures continue to reign supreme in our storybooks. From the graceful flight of dragons to the ethereal beauty of the Pegasus, these beings stir a sense of wonder and intrigue deep within us. Mythical creatures are depicted as symbols of power, mystery, and untamed potential. With these creatures, magic knows no limits!

The love for mythical creatures—and the love for things that are extraordinary—remains strong to this day. You may know a person who loves unicorns. Simply remove the wings from the Pegasus pattern (page 155) to make their dream come true! Some of the most advanced animals are in this chapter, but do not fear: They are still attainable! I've taken many different techniques throughout the book to create some of the more unique animals in this chapter, so don't worry about these patterns being too hard! Although these patterns may require more sewing and embellishments, I promise you that the result will be worth it.

# Sal the Stegosaurus

Dinosaurs are a childhood favorite! Although stegosaurus spikes are sharp and hard, this stegosaurus plushie is quite the opposite. You might have seen the plates and worried about the sewing they entailed. However, this pattern uses a simple technique to attach all of the spikes together to create one piece!

**Skill Level**
Intermediate

**Size**
Approx 15 inches (38 cm) long, 8 inches (20.5 cm) wide and 8 inches (20.5 cm) tall

**Yarn**
Super chunky chenille yarn, Premier Yarns Parfait Chunky, 100% polyester, 131 yds (120 m) and 3.5 oz (100 g) per skein

- Pale Blue (MC), 2 skeins, 262 yds (240 m) total

- Cornflower (C1), ½ skein, approx 66 yds (60 m) total

- Cream (C2), ½ skein, approx 66 yds (60 m) total

**Hooks**
US size H-8 (5mm)

**Notions**
Polyester fiberfill
Removable marker used to mark the first stitch of the round
Tapestry needle
Pair of 6mm safety eyes (optional)

**Gauge**
10 sc x 5 rounds = 4 inches (10 cm)

**Abbreviations**

**Blo** = back loop only
**C1** = color 1
**C2** = color 2
**Ch(s)** = chain(s)
**Dec** = decrease (crochet 2 sc together)
**Inc** = increase (work 2 sc into one stitch)
**MC** = main color
**Sc** = single crochet
**St(s)** = stitch(es)

## Legs (make 4)

With C1, ch 2 and inc 3 times in the 2nd ch away from hook (6 sts).

**Rnd 1:** Inc in each st (12 sts).

**Rnd 2:** Sc in the blo of each st (12 sts).

**Rnd 3:** With MC, sc in the blo of each st (12 sts). Break C1.

**Rnd 4:** Sc in each st (12 sts).

Fasten off and leave a 6-inch (15-cm) tail.

## Tail

With MC, ch 2 and inc 3 times in the 2nd ch away from hook (6 sts).

**Rnd 1:** Sc in each st (6 sts).

**Rnd 2:** (Inc, sc) 3 times (9 sts).

**Rnd 3:** (Inc, sc 2) 3 times (12 sts).

**Rnd 4:** (Inc, sc 3) 3 times (15 sts).

**Rnd 5:** (Inc, sc 4) 3 times (18 sts).

**Rnds 6–8:** Sc in each st (18 sts).

Fasten off and leave a 6-inch (15-cm) tail. Do not stuff.

## Body

With C2, ch 10. Inc in the 2nd ch from hook, sc in the next 7 chs, and inc 2 times in the last ch. Turn your work clockwise 180 degrees, so that you can work along the opposite side of the ch. Then, sc in the next 7 chs, and inc in the last ch (22 sts).

**Rnd 1:** Inc in the next 2 sts, sc 7, inc in the next 4 sc, sc 7, inc in the last 2 sts (30 sts).

**Rnd 2:** (Sc 2, attach Leg with 3 sts, sc 5, attach the next Leg with 3 sts, sc 2) 2 times (30 sts) (for more information on attaching legs, see page 10).

**Rnd 3:** With C2, sc 2. With MC, sc 9 remaining sts of the Leg. With C2, sc 5. With MC, sc 9 remaining sts of the Leg. With C2, sc 4. With MC, sc 9 remaining sts of the Leg. With C2, sc 5. With MC, sc 9 remaining sts of the Leg, sc 2 (54 sts). Break C2.

**Rnds 4–6:** With MC, sc in each st (54 sts).

**Rnd 7:** Sc 25, attach the Tail with 6 sts, sc 23 (54 sts).

**Rnd 8:** Sc in the first 25 sts of the Body, sc in the remaining 12 sts of the Tail, sc in the remaining 23 sts of the Body (60 sts).

**Rnd 9:** Sc 22, dec 3 times, sc 6, dec 3 times, sc 20 (54 sts).

**Rnds 10–11:** Sc in each st (54 sts).

**Rnd 12:** (Dec, sc 7) 6 times (48 sts).

**Rnd 13:** With MC, sc 13. With C1, sc 2. With MC, sc 4. With C1, sc 2. With MC, sc 11. With C1, sc 2. With MC, sc 5. With C1, sc 2. With MC, sc 7 (48 sts). Stuff the Legs and Tail.

**Rnd 14:** With MC, dec, sc 6, dec, sc 3. With C1, sc 3. With MC, dec, sc. With C1, sc 3. With MC, sc 2, dec, sc 5. With C1, sc, dec, sc. With MC, sc 4. With C1, sc, dec, sc. With MC, sc 5 (42 sts).

**Rnd 15:** With MC, sc 12. With C1, sc 2. With MC, sc 3. With C1, sc 2. With MC, sc 9. With C1, sc 2. With MC, sc 5. With C1, sc 2. With MC, sc 5 (42 sts). Start to lightly stuff the Body as you work.

**Rnd 16:** With MC, sc 31. With C1, sc 2. With MC, sc 9 (42 sts).

**Rnd 17:** With MC, (dec, sc 5) 2 times. With C1, dec, sc. With MC, sc 4, dec, sc 5, dec, sc. With C1, sc 3. With MC, sc, dec, sc 5 (36 sts).

**Rnd 18:** With MC, sc 12. With C1, sc 3. With MC, sc 12. With C1, sc 2. With MC, sc 7 (36 sts).

**Rnd 19:** With MC, (dec, sc 4) 2 times. With C1, dec, sc. With MC, sc 3, (dec, sc 4) 3 times (30 sts). Break C1.

**Rnd 20:** With MC, (dec, sc 3) 6 times (24 sts). Finish stuffing the Body.

**Rnd 21:** (Dec, sc 2) 6 times (18 sts).

**Rnd 22:** (Dec, sc) 6 times (12 sts).

**Rnd 23:** Dec 6 times (6 sts).

Fasten off and sew the hole closed.

## Head

With MC, ch 2 and inc 3 times in the 2nd ch away from hook (6 sts).

**Rnd 1:** Inc 6 times (12 sts).

**Rnd 2:** (Inc, sc) 6 times (18 sts).

**Rnd 3:** (Inc, sc 2) 6 times (24 sts).

**Rnds 4–8:** Sc in each st (24 sts). If using safety eyes, attach them on Rnd 5, 13 sts apart.

**Rnd 9:** (Dec, sc 2) 6 times (18 sts). Stuff the Head.

Fasten off and leave an 8-inch (20.5-cm) tail.

## Plate A (make 4)

With C1, ch 2, and inc 3 times in the 2nd ch away from hook (6 sts).

**Rnd 1:** Inc 6 times (12 sts).

**Rnd 2:** Sc in each st (12 sts).

Fasten off and leave a 3-inch (7.5-cm) tail. Do not stuff. (To see photos showing the process of creating the plates, refer to this technique used with Gale the Giraffe, page 59.)

## Plate B (make 1)

With C1, ch 2, and inc 3 times in the 2nd ch away from hook (6 sts).

**Rnd 1:** Sc in each st (6 sts).

Fasten off and leave a 3-inch (7.5-cm) tail. Do not stuff.

## Plate C (make 2)

With C1, ch 2, and sc 6 into the second ch away from hook (6 sts).

**Rnd 1:** (Inc, sc 2) 2 times (8 sts).

Fasten off the 1st Plate C and leave a 3-inch (7.5-cm) tail. Do not fasten off the 2nd Plate C. Instead, ch 1, fold the Plate in half, and sc across both sides.

Then (fold one Plate A in half, place your hook into the 1st and 12th st of the Plate, and sc across both sides) and repeat for each Plate A. Fold the 1st Plate C in half, place your hook into the 1st and 8th st of this Plate, and sc across both sides. Fold Plate B in half, place your hook into the 1st and 6th st of this Plate, and sc across both sides (35 sts) (for more information on sc across both sides, see Gale the Giraffe, page 59).

Fasten off and leave a 12-inch (30.5-cm) tail. Do not stuff.

## Assembly

Sew the Head to the front of the Body on Rnds 7–12. Then, align the line of Plates across the middle of the body in this order: Both Plate Cs at the tail, then all 4 Plate As, then Plate B at the top just behind the head. Sew the Plates onto the Body. Weave in all ends.

If you prefer to embroider the eyes instead of using safety eyes, set them 13 sts apart on Rnd 5 of the Head (for more information on embroidering eyes, see page 13).

# Dio the Dragon

This dragon (and his pattern) may seem frightening at first, but with patience you can learn how to bring him to life using a Puff stitch for his wings, embroidery for his scales and a slip stitch for his tail. With a lot of techniques comes a lot of pieces, and more sewing than you've probably seen in the majority of the patterns in this book. If you're looking for the biggest challenge, look no further.

**Skill Level**
Advanced

**Size**
Approx 14 inches (35.5 cm) long, 7 inches (18 cm) wide and 12 inches (30.5 cm) tall

**Yarn**
Super chunky chenille yarn, Premier Yarns Parfait Chunky, 100% polyester, 131 yds (120 m) and 3.5 oz (100 g) per skein

- Cardinal (MC), 2 skeins, 262 yds (240 m) total
- Cream (C1), ½ skein, approx 66 yds (60 m) total
- Ruby (C2), ½ skein, approx 66 yds (60 m) total

**Hooks**
US size H-8 (5mm)

**Notions**
Polyester fiberfill
Removable marker used to mark the first stitch of the round
Tapestry needle
Pair of 6mm safety eyes (optional)

**Gauge**
10 sc x 5 rounds = 4 inches (10 cm)

### Abbreviations
**C1** = color 1
**C2** = color 2
**Ch(s)** = chain(s)
**Dec** = decrease
(crochet 2 sc together)
**Flo** = front loop only
**Inc** = increase (work 2 sc into one stitch)
**MC** = main color
**Sc** = single crochet
**Sl st** = slip stitch
**St(s)** = stitch(es)

### Pattern Stitches
**Puff Stitch** = Yarn over, insert your hook through the st, yarn over and then draw up a loop. Repeat until you have 6 loops on the hook. Yarn over and draw through all 6 loops.

## Front Legs (make 2)

With MC, ch 2 and inc 3 times in the 2nd ch away from hook (6 sts).

**Rnd 1:** Inc 6 times (12 sts).

**Rnd 2:** Inc, sc, dec 2 times, sc 5, inc (12 sts).

**Rnds 3–6:** Sc in each st (12 sts).

Fasten off and leave a 3-inch (7.5-cm) tail. Do not stuff.

## Right Back Leg

With MC, ch 2 and inc 3 times in the 2nd ch away from hook (6 sts).

**Rnd 1:** Inc 6 times (12 sts).

**Rnds 2–3:** Inc, sc 3, dec 2 times, sc 3, inc (12 sts).

**Rnd 4:** Sc 4, inc 4 times in the flo, sc 4 (16 sts).

**Rnds 5–7:** Sc in each st (16 sts).

**Rnd 8:** Sc 3. Leave the remaining 13 sts untouched for proper leg placement (16 sts).

Fasten off and leave a 3-inch (7.5-cm) tail. Do not stuff.

## Left Back Leg

With MC, ch 2 and inc 3 times in the 2nd ch away from hook (6 sts).

**Rnd 1:** Inc 6 times (12 sts).

**Rnds 2–3:** Inc, sc 3, dec 2 times, sc 3, inc (12 sts).

**Rnd 4:** Sc 4, inc 4 times in the flo, sc 4 (16 sts).

**Rnds 5–7:** Sc in each st (16 sts).

**Rnd 8:** Sc 10. Leave the remaining 6 sts untouched for proper Leg placement (16 sts).

Fasten off and leave a 3-inch (7.5-cm) tail. Do not stuff.

## Head

With MC, ch 2 and inc 3 times in the 2nd ch away from hook (6 sts).

**Rnd 1:** Inc 6 times (12 sts).

**Rnd 2:** (Inc, sc) 6 times (18 sts).

**Rnd 3:** (Inc, sc 2) 6 times (24 sts).

**Rnd 4:** (Inc, sc 3) 6 times (30 sts).

**Rnds 5–9:** Sc in each st (30 sts).

Fasten off and leave a 3-inch (7.5-cm) tail. Do not stuff.

## Tail

With MC, ch 2 and inc 3 times in the 2nd ch away from hook (6 sts).

**Rnd 1:** (Inc, sc) 3 times (9 sts).

**Rnd 2:** (Inc, sc 2) 3 times (12 sts).

**Rnd 3:** (Inc, sc 3) 3 times (15 sts).

**Rnd 4:** (Inc, sc 4) 3 times (18 sts).

**Rnd 5:** Place your hook into the 1st and 18th st (3 sts on hook) (image 1). Sl st the sts together. Repeat this for the 2nd and 17th st, and the 3rd and the 16th st (image 2). Sc in the 4th st. Sc in the next 5 sts of the Tail (image 3). Place your hook into the 9th and the 10th st (3 sts on hook). Sl st the stitches together. Repeat this for the 8th and 11th st, and the 7th and 12th st. Sc in the 13th st (image 4). Sc in the remaining 2 sts. Sc in the 4th st. This is the start of the new Rnd. Sc in the remaining 5 sts (6 sts).

**Rnd 6:** With MC, sc. With C1, sc 2. With MC, sc 3 (6 sts).

**Rnd 7:** With MC, sc. With C1, sc 3. With MC, sc 2 (6 sts).

**Rnd 8:** With MC, inc, sc. With C1, inc, sc. With MC, inc, sc (9 sts).

**Rnd 9:** With MC, sc 3. With C1, sc 3. With MC, sc 3 (9 sts).

**Rnd 10:** With MC, inc, sc 2, inc. With C1, sc 2, inc. With MC, sc 2 (12 sts).

**Rnd 11:** With MC, sc 7. With C1, sc 3. With MC, sc 2 (12 sts).

**Rnd 12:** With MC, sc 8. With C1, sc 2. With MC, sc 2 (12 sts).

**Rnd 13:** With MC, (inc, sc) 4 times. With C1, inc, sc, inc. With MC, sc (18 sts).

**Rnd 14:** With MC, (inc, sc 2) 4 times, inc. With C1, sc 2, inc, sc. With MC, sc (24 sts).

**Rnd 15:** With MC, sc. Leave the remaining 23 sts unworked for proper Tail attachment later (24 sts).

Fasten off and leave a 3-inch (7.5-cm) tail. Do not stuff.

## Body

With C1, ch 10. Inc in the 2nd ch from hook, sc in the next 7 ch, and inc 2 times in the last ch. Turn your work clockwise 180 degrees, so that you can work along the opposite side of the ch. Then, sc in the next 7 chs, and inc in the last ch (22 sts).

**Rnd 1:** Inc in the first 2 sts, sc 7, inc in the next 4 sts, sc 7, inc in the last 2 sts (30 sts).

**Rnd 2:** Sc in each st (30 sts).

**Rnd 3:** Sc 2, attach Front Leg with 3 sts, sc 5, attach Right Back Leg with 4 sts, sc 4, attach Left Back Leg with 4 sts, sc 5, attach Front Leg with 3 sts (30 sts) (for more information on attaching legs, see page 10).

**Rnd 4:** With C1, sc in the next 2 sts of the Body. With MC, sc in the remaining 9 sts of the Front Leg. With C1, sc in the next 5 sts of the Body. With MC, sc in the remaining 12 sts of the Right Back Leg. With C1, sc in the next 4 sts of the Body. With MC, sc in the remaining 12 sts of the Left Back Leg. With C1, sc in the next 5 sts of the Body. With MC, sc in the remaining 9 sts of the Front Leg (58 sts).

**Rnd 5:** With C1, sc 5. With MC, sc 23, attach Tail with 5 sts, sc 22. With C1, sc 3 (58 sts).

**Rnd 6:** With C1, sc 5. With MC, sc 23, sc 19 in the remaining sts of the Tail, then sc into the next 22 Body sts. With C1, sc 3 (72 sts).

**Rnd 7:** With C1, sc 6. With MC, sc 22, dec, sc 17, dec, sc 21. With C1, sc 2 (70 sts).

**Rnd 8:** With C1, sc 6. With MC, sc 22, dec, sc 13, dec, sc 23. With C1, sc 2 (68 sts).

**Rnd 9:** With C1, sc 7. With MC, sc 17, dec 4 times, sc 11, dec 4 times, sc 15. With C1, sc 2 (60 sts).

**Rnds 10–11:** With C1, sc 7. With MC, sc 52. With C1, sc (60 sts).

**Rnd 12:** With C1, sc 8. With MC, sc 11, (dec, sc 3) 6 times, sc 10. With C1, sc (54 sts).

**Rnd 13:** With C1, sc 8. With MC, sc 46 (54 sts).

**Rnd 14:** With C1, sc 8. With MC, sc 11, (dec, sc 2) 6 times, sc 11 (48 sts).

**Rnd 15:** With C1, sc 9. With MC, sc 39 (48 sts).

**Rnd 16:** With C1, sc 9. With MC, sc 11, (dec, sc) 6 times, sc 10 (42 sts).

**Rnd 17:** With MC, sc. With C1, sc 8. With MC, sc 33 (42 sts).

**Rnd 18:** With MC, sc. With C1, sc 9. With MC, sc 9, dec 6 times, sc 11 (36 sts).

**Rnd 19:** With MC, sc. With C1, sc 9. With MC, sc 12. Place your hook into the flo of the 22nd and 23rd st (3 sts on hook). Sl st the sts together. Repeat this for the 24th and 21st st, the 25th and 20th st, the 26th and 19th st, the 27th and 18th st, the 28th and 17th st, and the 29th and 16th st (for more information on closing off a body, see Flynn the Fox, page 29). Sc in the 30th st. Sc in the remaining 6 sts of this Rnd and in the first 16 sts of the next Rnd, sc 2. With C1, sc 8. With MC, sc 6. This is the new beginning of the Rnd (22 sts). Stuff the Body. Overstuff the Body on Rnds 18–21.

**Rnd 20:** With MC, sc 9. With C1, sc 7. With MC, sc 6 (22 sts).

**Rnds 21–22:** With MC, sc 9. With C1, sc 8. With MC, sc 5 (22 sts).

**Rnd 23:** With MC, sc 10. With C1, sc 7. With MC, sc 5 (22 sts). Break C1.

**Rnd 24:** With MC, sc 10, attach the Head with 7 sts, sc 5 (22 sts). Stuff the Neck lightly as you work.

**Rnd 25:** Sc in the first 10 sts of the Neck, sc in the remaining 23 sts of the Head, sc in the remaining 5 sts of the Neck (38 sts). If using safety eyes, attach them on this round, 18 sts apart on Rd 5 of the Head now.

**Rnd 26:** Sc 7, dec 3 times, sc 17, dec 3 times, sc 2 (32 sts).

**Rnd 27:** Sc 7, dec 2 times, sc 15, dec 2 times, sc 2 (28 sts).

**Rnd 28:** Sc in each st (28 sts). Stuff the Head.

**Rnd 29:** (Dec, sc 2) 7 times (21 sts).

**Rnd 30:** Sc in each st (21 sts).

**Rnd 31:** (Dec, sc) 7 times (14 sts).

**Rnd 32:** Dec 7 times (7 sts). Finish stuffing the Neck.

Fasten off and sew the hole closed.

## Plates (make 9)

With C2, ch 2 and inc 3 times in the 2nd ch away from hook (6 sts).

**Rnd 1:** (Sc 2, inc) 2 times (8 sts).

**Rnd 2:** Sc in each st (8 sts).

Fasten off the first 8 Plates and leave a 3-inch (7.5-cm) tail. Do not fasten off the 9th Plate. Instead, ch 1, fold the Plate in half, and sc across both sides.

Then taking the next Plate, fold in half, place your hook into the 1st and 8th st of the Plate, and sc across both sides. Repeat with each Plate (28 sts) (for more information on sc across both sides, see Gale the Giraffe, page 59).

Fasten off and leave a 12-inch (30.5-cm) tail. Do not stuff.

## Front Plates (make 2)

With C2, ch 2 and inc 3 times in the 2nd ch away from hook (6 sts).

**Rnd 1:** (Inc, sc 2) 2 times (8 sts).

**Rnd 2:** (Inc, sc, inc, Puff st) 2 times (12 sts).

**Rnd 3:** Sc in each st (12 sts).

**Rnd 4:** (Dec, sc) 4 times (8 sts).

**Rnd 5:** Dec 4 times (4 sts).

Fold the Front Plate flat. Fasten off and leave a 12-inch (30.5-cm) tail. Do not stuff.

## Wings (make 2)

With C2, ch 2 and inc 3 times in the 2nd ch away from hook (6 sts).

**Rnd 1:** Sc in each st (6 sts).

**Rnd 2:** (Inc, sc) 3 times (9 sts).

**Rnd 3:** (Inc, sc 2) 3 times (12 sts).

**Rnd 4:** Sc in each st (12 sts).

**Rnd 5:** (Inc, sc 3) 3 times (15 sts).

**Rnd 6:** (Inc, sc 4) 3 times (18 sts).

**Rnd 7:** (Inc, sc 5) 3 times (21 sts).

**Rnd 8:** (Inc, sc 6) 3 times (24 sts).

**Rnd 9:** (Inc, sc 7) 3 times (27 sts).

**Rnd 10:** Dec, sc 7, dec, Puff st, sc 6, dec, sc 7 (24 sts).

**Rnd 11:** (Dec, sc 6) 3 times (21 sts).

**Rnd 12:** (Dec, sc 5) 3 times (18 sts).

**Rnd 13:** (Dec, sc 4) 3 times (15 sts).

**Rnd 14:** (Dec, sc 3) 3 times (12 sts).

**Rnd 15:** Sc in each st (12 sts).

**Rnd 16:** (Dec, sc 2) 3 times (9 sts).

**Rnd 17:** (Dec, sc) 3 times (6 sts).

Fold the Wing flat. Fasten off and leave a 12-inch (30.5-cm) tail. Do not stuff.

## Assembly

Sew Rnd 17 of the Wings to the side of the Body on Rnds 15–16. Sew the Front Plates to the side of the Head, 20 sts apart. Sew the Plates to the back of the Body, with the first Plate sewn on Rnd 7 of the Tail and the last on Rnd 6 of the Head. Weave in all ends.

With MC, embroider a line alongside the top of the Wing, to make an upside-down V-shape on the top of the Wing. Then, embroider a vertical line in between the intersection of the two lines embroidered previously. The line should end at the bottom of the Wing.

If you prefer to embroider the eyes instead of using safety eyes, set them on Rnd 5 of the Head, 18 sts apart (for more information on embroidering eyes, see page 13).

# Percy the Pegasus

If you believe in magic, this pegasus is for you. If you enjoyed making Henry the Horse, this horse is one step up: He gets wings! The wings are made with a simple increasing technique—and then you fold the wings flat. Add a horn for a magical touch!

## Skill Level
Intermediate

## Size
Approx 16 inches (40.5 cm) long, 8 inches (20.5 cm) wide and 14 inches (35.5 cm) tall

## Yarn
Super chunky chenille yarn, Premier Yarns Parfait Chunky, 100% polyester, 131 yds (120 m) and 3.5 oz (100 g) per skein

- Cream (MC), 2 skeins, 262 yds (240 m) total
- Mustard (C1), ½ skein, approx 66 yds (60 m) total
- Pale Gray (C2), 1 yd (1 m) total

## Hooks
US size H-8 (5mm)

## Notions
Polyester fiberfill
Removable marker to mark beginning of round
Tapestry needle
Pair of 10mm safety eyes (optional)

## Gauge
10 sc x 5 rounds = 4 inches (10 cm)

## Abbreviations
**Blo** = back loop only
**C1** = color 1
**C2** = color 2
**Ch(s)** = chain(s)
**Dec** = decrease (crochet 2 sc together)
**Flo** = front loop only
**Inc** = increase (work 2 sc into one stitch)
**MC** = main color
**Sc** = single crochet
**Sl st** = slip stitch
**St(s)** = stitch(es)

## Legs (make 4)

With C1, ch 2 and inc 3 times in the 2nd ch away from hook (6 sts).

**Rnd 1:** Inc in each st (12 sts).

**Rnd 2:** Sc in the blo of each st (12 sts).

**Rnds 3–7:** With MC, sc in each st (12 sts).

Fasten off and leave a 6-inch (15-cm) tail for sewing.

## Tail

With C1, ch 2 and inc 3 times in the 2nd ch away from hook (6 sts).

**Rnds 1–2:** Sc in each st (6 sts).

**Rnds 3–5:** Dec 2 times, inc 2 times in the flo (6 sts).

**Rnd 6:** Inc 6 times (12 sts).

**Rnds 7–12:** Sc in each st (12 sts).

**Rnd 13:** (Dec, sc) 4 times (8 sts). Stuff the Tail.

**Rnds 14–17:** Sc in each st (8 sts).

**Rnd 18:** Ch 1. Fold the Tail in half side to side, and sc across through both sides (4 sts) (for more information on sc across both sides, see Gale the Giraffe, page 59).

Fasten off and leave a 6-inch (15-cm) tail for sewing.

## Ears (make 2)

With MC, ch 2 and inc 3 times in the 2nd ch away from hook (6 sts).

**Rnd 1:** Sc in each st (6 sts).

**Rnd 2:** Inc 6 times (12 sts).

Fasten off and leave a 6-inch (15-cm) tail for sewing.

## Head

With MC, ch 2 and inc 3 times in the 2nd ch away from hook (6 sts).

**Rnd 1:** Inc 6 times (12 sts).

**Rnd 2:** (Inc, sc) 6 times (18 sts).

**Rnds 3–5:** Sc in each st (18 sts).

**Rnd 6:** Sc 9, inc in the flo in the next 6 sts, sc 3 (24 sts).

**Rnd 7:** Sc 9, (inc, sc) 6 times, sc 3 (30 sts).

**Rnd 8:** Sc in each st (30 sts). If using safety eyes, attach them on this round, 15 sts apart on st 11 and st 26.

Fasten off and leave a 6-inch (15-cm) tail.

## Body

With MC, ch 13. Inc in the 2nd ch from hook, sc in the next 10 chs, and inc 2 times in the last ch. Turn your work clockwise 180 degrees, so that you can work along the opposite side of the ch. Then sc in the next 10 chs, and inc in the last ch (28 sts).

**Rnd 1:** Inc in the next 2 sts, sc 10, inc in the next 4 sts, sc 10, inc in the next 2 sts (36 sts).

**Rnd 2:** (Sc 2, attach Leg with 3 sts, sc 8, attach the next Leg with 3 sts, sc 2) 2 times (36 sts) (for more information on attaching legs, see page 10).

**Rnd 3:** (Sc in the next 2 sts of the Body, sc in the remaining 9 sts of the next Leg, sc in the next 8 sts of the Body, sc in the remaining 9 sts of the next Leg, sc in the next 2 sts of the Body) 2 times (60 sts).

**Rnds 4–10:** Sc in each st (60 sts).

**Rnd 11:** Sc 30, attach the Tail with 4 sts, sc 26 (60 sts).

**Rnd 12:** Sc in each st (60 sts).

**Rnd 13:** (Dec, sc 8) 6 times (54 sts).

**Rnds 14–16:** Sc in each st (54 sts).

**Rnd 17:** (Dec, sc 7) 6 times (48 sts).

**Rnd 18:** (Dec, sc 6) 6 times (42 sts).

**Rnd 19:** Sc 13, (dec, sc 2) 6 times, sc 5 (36 sts). Stuff lightly as you work.

**Rnd 20:** Sc 13, (dec, sc) 6 times, sc 5 (30 sts).

**Rnd 21:** Sc 13, work 6 dec, sc 5 (24 sts).

**Rnd 22:** Sc 15. Place your hook into the flo of the 16th and 17th st (3 sts on hook). Sl st the sts together. Repeat this for the 18th and 15th st, the 19th and 14th st, the 20th and 13th st, and the 21st and 12th st (for more information on closing off a body, see Flynn the Fox, page 29). Inc in the 22nd st. Sc in the remaining 2 sts of this Rnd and the first 11 sts of the next Rnd. This is the new beginning of the Rnd (15 sts). Stuff the Body. Overstuff the Body on Rnds 18–21.

**Rnds 23–24:** Sc in each st (15 sts). This is the Neck portion.

**Rnd 25:** Sc 6, attach the Head with 6 sts, sc 3 (15 sts).

**Rnd 26:** In the next sts of the Neck, sc 4, dec. In the remaining sts of the Head, dec, sc 20, dec. In the remaining sts of the Neck, dec, sc (29 sts).

**Rnd 27:** Sc 13, dec, sc 14 (28 sts).

**Rnd 28:** Sc in each st (28 sts).

**Rnd 29:** (Dec, sc 2) 7 times (21 sts).

**Rnd 30:** Sc in each st (21 sts). Stuff the Head and Neck.

**Rnd 31:** (Dec, sc) 7 times (14 sts).

**Rnd 32:** Dec 7 times (7 sts).

Fasten off and sew the hole closed.

## Mane

With C1, ch 2 and inc 3 times in the 2nd ch away from hook (6 sts).

**Rnd 1:** Sc in each st (6 sts).

**Rnds 3–5:** Dec 2 times. Inc 2 times in the flo (6 sts).

**Rnd 6:** (Inc, sc) 3 times (9 sts).

**Rnds 7–9:** Sc in each st (9 sts).

**Rnd 10:** (Inc, sc 2) 3 times (12 sts).

**Rnds 11–12:** Sc in each st (12 sts).

**Rnd 13:** (Inc, sc 3) 3 times (15 sts).

**Rnds 14–18:** Sc in each st (15 sts).

**Rnd 19:** (Dec, sc 3) 3 times (12 sts). Only stuff Rnds 3–17.

**Rnds 20–23:** Sc in each st (12 sts).

**Rnd 24:** (Dec, sc) 4 times (8 sts).

**Rnds 25–26:** Sc in each st (8 sts).

**Rnd 27:** Ch 1. Fold the Tail in half side to side, and sc across through both sides (4 sts) (for more information on sc across both sides, see Gale the Giraffe, page 59).

Fasten off and leave a 6-inch (15-cm) tail for sewing.

## Forelock

With C1, ch 2 and inc 3 times in the 2nd ch away from hook (6 sts).

**Rnd 1:** Sc in each st (6 sts).

**Rnds 3–5:** Dec 2 times. Inc 2 in the flo (6 sts).

**Rnd 6:** Inc 6 times (12 sts).

**Rnds 7–9:** Sc in each st (12 sts). Stuff the Forelock.

**Rnd 10:** Dec 6 times (6 sts).

Fasten off and sew the hole closed. Leave a 6-inch (15-cm) tail for sewing.

## Horn

With C2, ch 2 and inc 3 times in the 2nd ch away from hook (6 sts).

**Rnd 1:** Sc in each st (6 sts).

**Rnd 2:** (Inc, sc) 3 times (9 sts).

**Rnds 3–5:** Sc in each st (9 sts).

Fasten off and leave a 6-inch (15-cm) tail for sewing.

## Wings (make 2)

With MC, ch 2 and inc 3 times in the 2nd ch away from hook (6 sts).

**Rnds 1–3:** Sc in each st (6 sts).

**Rnd 4:** Inc in the flo of the next 4 sts, sc 2 (10 sts).

**Rnd 5:** (Inc, sc) 4 times, sc 2 (14 sts).

**Rnd 6:** Sc in each st (14 sts).

**Rnd 7:** Sc 4, (dec, sc) 2 times, sc 4 (12 sts).

**Rnd 8:** Sc 4, inc in the flo of the next 4 sts, sc 4 (16 sts).

**Rnd 9:** Sc in each st (16 sts).

**Rnd 10:** Dec, sc 12, dec (14 sts).

**Rnd 11:** Sc 5, dec 2 times, sc 5 (12 sts).

**Rnd 12:** Sc in each st (12 sts).

**Rnd 13:** Dec 6 times (6 sts).

Fasten off and sew the hole closed. Leave a 6-inch (15-cm) tail for sewing. Do not stuff. For images on the process for making wings, refer to Cara the Chicken on page 105 or Bibi the Bird on page 77.

## Assembly

Sew Rnd 25 of the Mane to Rnd 28 of the Body. Curve the Mane so that the end lies on the left side of the Neck, and sew Rnd 4 of the Mane to Rnd 19 of the Body. Sew each Ear to Rnd 27 of the Body. Sew the Horn to the top of the Head, between each Ear. Sew Rnds 1–3 of each Wing to Rnds 17–19 of the Body. Finally, sew the Forelock to the top of the Head, in front of the Ears. Weave in all ends.

If you prefer to embroider the eyes instead of using safety eyes, set them 15 sts apart on Rnd 8 of the Head (for more information on sewing eyes onto plushies, see page 13).

# Pyria the Phoenix

The phoenix is a mythical, immortal bird made of fire—it's surely an amazing creature! Pyria the Phoenix is one of the most colorful patterns in the book, and the wings are the best part to make! Although I sewed the wings inward, feel free to sew the wings outward, as if the bird is flying away.

**Skill Level**
Advanced

**Size**
Approx 7 inches (18 cm) long, 7 inches (18 cm) wide and 14 inches (35.5 cm) tall

**Yarn**
Super chunky chenille yarn, Premier Yarns Parfait Chunky, 100% polyester, 131 yds (120 m) and 3.5 oz (100 g) per skein

- Poppy (MC), 2 skeins, 262 yds (240 m) total
- Tangerine (C1), ½ skein, approx 66 yds (60 m) total
- Sunshine (C2), ⅓ skein, 44 yds (40 m) total

**Hooks**
US size H-8 (5mm)

**Notions**
Polyester fiberfill
Removable marker used to mark the first stitch of the round
Tapestry needle
Pair of 10mm safety eyes (optional)

**Gauge**
10 sc x 5 rounds = 4 inches (10 cm)

## Abbreviations

**C1** = color 1
**C2** = color 2
**Ch(s)** = chain(s)
**Dec** = decrease (crochet 2 sc together)
**Flo** = front loop only
**Inc** = increase (work 2 sc into one stitch)
**MC** = main color
**Sc** = single crochet
**St(s)** = stitch(es)

## Pattern Stitches

**Puff Stitch** = Yarn over, insert your hook through the st, yarn over and then draw up a loop. Repeat until you have 6 loops on the hook. Yarn over and draw through all 6 loops.

## Tail Feathers (make 3)

With MC, ch 8. Inc in the 2nd ch from hook, sc in the next 5 ch, and inc 2 times in the last ch. Turn your work clockwise 180 degrees, so that you can work along the opposite side of the ch. Then, sc in the next 5 chs, and inc in the last ch (18 sts).

**Rnd 1:** Inc in the next 2 sts, sc 5, inc in the next 4 sts, sc 5, inc in the next 2 sts (26 sts).

**Rnd 2:** (Sc in the next st of the Feather, ch 3, sc in the next st of the Feather) 13 times (26 sts).

Fasten off and leave a 6-inch (15-cm) tail for sewing.

## Beak

With C2, ch 2, and inc 2 times in the 2nd ch away from hook (4 sts).

**Rnd 1:** (Inc, sc) 2 times (6 sts).

**Rnd 2:** Sc 2, inc in the flo of the next 3 sts, sc (9 sts).

Fasten off and leave a 6-inch (15-cm) tail for sewing.

## Wings (make 2)

With MC, ch 2 and inc 3 times in the 2nd ch away from hook (6 sts).

**Rnd 1:** Sc in each st (6 sts).

**Rnd 2:** Inc in each st (12 sts).

**Rnd 3:** Sc 3. Ch 2 and inc 3 times in the 2nd ch from hook. (This is a Wing feather.) Sc in the remaining 9 sts of the Wing (12 sts).

**Rnd 4:** Inc 12 times (24 sts). When working around the feathers in this row and the following rows, make sure that the feather is in front of the hook when you work into the next st to allow it to lie flat (see images 1–4 on the next page, which show Rnd 10).

**Rnd 5:** Sc 2. Ch 2 and inc 3 times in the 2nd ch from hook. Sc in the next 5 sts of the Wing. Ch 2 and inc 3 times in the 2nd ch from hook. Sc in the remaining 17 sts of the Wing (24 sts). Break MC.

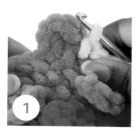  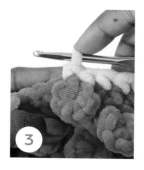 

**Rnd 6:** With C1, (inc, sc 3) 6 times (30 sts).

**Rnd 7:** Sc 3. Ch 2 and inc 3 times in the 2nd ch from hook. (Sc in the next 5 sts of the Wing. Ch 2 and inc 3 times in the 2nd ch from hook) 2 times. Sc in the remaining 17 sts of the Wing (30 sts).

**Rnd 8:** Sc in each st (30 sts). When working around the row, make sure that the feathers are in front of the hook when you work into the next st to allow them to lie flat.

**Rnd 9:** Sc 6. Ch 2 and inc 3 times in the 2nd ch from hook. Sc in the next 5 sts of the Wing. Ch 2 and inc 3 times in the 2nd ch from hook. Sc in the remaining 19 sts of the Wing (30 sts). Break C1.

**Rnd 10:** With C2, sc in each st (30 sts). When working around the row, make sure that the feathers are in front of the hook when you work into the next st to allow them to lie flat.

**Rnd 11:** Sc 3. Ch 2 and inc 3 times in the 2nd ch from hook. (Sc in the next 6 sts of the Wing. Ch 2 and inc 3 times in the 2nd ch from hook) 2 times. Sc in the remaining 15 sts of the Wing (30 sts).

**Rnd 12:** Ch 1. Place your hook into the 1st and 30th st and sc across both sides.

Fasten off and leave a 6-inch (15-cm) tail for sewing. Do not stuff.

## Head and Body

With MC, ch 2 and inc 3 times in the 2nd ch away from hook (6 sts).

**Rnd 1:** (Inc, sc 2) 2 times (8 sts).

**Rnd 2:** (Inc, sc, inc, Puff st) 2 times (12 sts).

**Rnd 3:** Sc in each st (12 sts).

**Rnd 4:** (Dec, sc) 4 times (8 sts).

**Rnd 5:** Sc in each st (8 sts).

**Rnd 6:** Inc 8 times in the flo (16 sts).

**Rnd 7:** (Inc, sc) 8 times (24 sts).

**Rnd 8:** (Inc, sc 3) 6 times (30 sts).

**Rnd 9:** (Inc, sc 4) 6 times (36 sts).

**Rnds 10–15:** Sc in each st (36 sts). If using safety eyes, attach them on Rnd 13 on the 14th and 21st st.

**Rnd 16:** (Dec, sc 4) 6 times (30 sts).

**Rnd 17:** Sc in each st (30 sts). Stuff the Head.

**Rnd 18:** (Dec, sc 3) 6 times (24 sts).

**Rnd 19:** (Dec, sc 2) 6 times (18 sts).

**Rnd 20:** In the flo, (inc, sc 2) 6 times (24 sts).

**Rnd 21:** Sc 6, inc 6 times, sc 12 (30 sts).

**Rnd 22:** Sc in each st (30 sts).

**Rnd 23:** (Inc, sc 4) 6 times (36 sts).

**Rnds 24–28:** Sc in each st (36 sts).

**Rnd 29:** Sc 8, (dec, sc) 6 times, sc 10 (30 sts). Stuff the Body.

**Rnd 30:** Sc in each st (30 sts).

**Rnd 31:** Sc 9, dec 6 times, sc 9 (24 sts).

**Rnds 32–35:** Sc in each st (24 sts).

**Rnd 36:** (Dec, sc 2) 6 times (18 sts).

**Rnd 37:** (Dec, sc) 6 times (12 sts).

**Rnds 38–40:** Sc in each st (12 sts).

**Rnd 41:** Dec 6 times (6 sts). Finish stuffing the Body.

Fasten off and sew the hole closed.

## Assembly

Sew each Wing to opposite sides of the Body, sewing the first 3 sts of the last Rnd of each Wing on Rnd 21 of the Body, 15 sts apart. Make sure that the Rnd 1 of each Wing face each other. Sew the Tail Feathers to Rnd 38 of the Body, 2 sts apart. Sew the Beak on Rnds 13–15 of the Head, in the middle. Weave in all ends.

If you prefer to embroider the eyes instead of using safety eyes, set them 2 sts apart from each side of the Beak on Rnd 13 of the Head (for more information on sewing eyes onto plushies, see page 13).

# Acknowledgments

Thank you to my mom and dad for their consistent support and appreciation for my craft—even when I didn't feel as confident.

I thank all of my siblings: Samuel, Ayo, Elizabeth, Abraham, Benjamin, John and Grace for testing my plushies. I know that they are perfect for cuddles thanks to all of you!

Special thanks to my pattern testers. This book wouldn't be as successful without your critique.

Thanks to my tech editor Cathy. She caught a lot (and I mean a lot) of errors.

Thank you to Katherine, Sarah and the rest of the team at Page Street. I almost deleted the email proposing the book deal—and I'm glad I didn't.

And last but not least, I thank God for providing me with this incredible opportunity and the mind to be able to see it through.

# About the Author

**Glory Shofowora,** also known on social media as Crafting in Glory, has grown up crocheting and working with every craft medium available. Although she's crocheted a lot of different items, she's been crocheting unique stuffed animals and plushies and sharing her passion since 2021.

She is currently working on her bachelor's degree in education. When she's not crocheting, she's playing online games with her siblings. You can find her on Instagram and TikTok @CraftingInGlory or her website www.craftinglory.com.

# Index